BEAUTY
CLIENTS FOR LIFE

How To Foster New Business
Relationships Using Social Media

By
Melissa Liscio

Edited by **Chelle Johnson**
Design by Jorge Luis Barboza
Published by Mimic Print

ISBN-13: 978-1542601825
ISBN-10: 1542601827

I would like to dedicate this book to my business and life partner, Ovi Almasan. The truth is this book wouldn't exist if it weren't for you.

Writing Beauty Clients For Life was a long journey filled with love, dedication, hard work, extreme execution, and, truth be told, anxiety for this book to be perfect for the thousands of beauty professionals who will go on to read it.

Thank you for always standing by me and executing on our crazy ideas we have for the future.

About the Author

After years as a hairstylist behind the chair, Melissa's love for the industry nudged her to dream bigger and focus her efforts exclusively on educating and coaching hair professionals around the world on digital marketing and salon business development. Melissa lives in Toronto, Canada.

Table of Content

Forward: Adapt or Be Left Behind

If you're reading this book you're in luck because there are over 1.2 million hairstylists on social media in the U.S alone, and this version of the book has only been printed a few thousand times. So if you're concerned everyone has access to this information, worry no more. You and only a handful of other beauty professionals do.

I kindly ask that you leave your current opinions about social media at the door and open your mind to this knowledge. I also ask that before you dismiss the information in this book you try to make it work for yourself and that you do so more than once. You may fail a few times but you may also succeed on the first try. Either way, it won't happen overnight, but it will happen if you try hard enough.

This book is dedicated to and written for the beauty professional with an endless thirst for growth and learning - the hairstylist, cosmetologist, or make-up artist who wants to further grow their clientele and business using social media. Whether we like it or not, social media is a necessary evil to each and every industry, including our own.

Heck, even politics depends on social media nowadays.

There is no fluff in this book; it could have been twice as long, but it's not. In fact, it's raw and to the point. Having said that, some of the online information available to our industry is outdated - please know I did my best to include advice and actionable steps that are evergreen (and last beyond any algorithm change).

Everyone's time is limited, and I am hyper-aware of the fact I only have a few moments to gain your attention and keep it. In a world where the common misconception is that bigger is better, I believe less is more. In these next 22 chapters you will find one woman's informed opinion on each topic I found necessary to address so that you're armed with enough information to do something about the future and not be left behind. I have interacted with over 20,000 hairstylists since starting Hairstylist Tribe, and these chapters answer the top 22 most common questions I have received from these professionals.

I don't want your business to be just another statistic. The hair school I attended 10 years ago is now a carpet superstore. And my old beauty school isn't the only one. I have traveled to over 40 states in the US over the last 3 years and have driven by plenty of salons and beauty schools with a "For Lease" sign in the window, including the upscale salon franchise I worked for. Social media itself isn't killing businesses like beauty schools and salons. The lack of adaptation on the part of the owners of these businesses is. This book will prepare you to ride the social media wave that is already happening. I'm confident that applying these concepts will increase your chances of surfing the wave rather than being pulled in by the undertow. So let's get started!

CHAPTER 1

You Don't Need Anyone's Permission

This book never would have happened had I gone around asking for others' permission to write it. I gave myself permission. I didn't ask family, I didn't ask friends, and I didn't ask my colleagues when I quit my salon career to start building a marketing and branding business for the beauty industry.

The tipping point for me was when I was considering leaving my full-time job. In the year leading up to my salon exit, I would sit in the back room during the slow times consuming audio books and taking notes. I prepared myself to give myself permission to leave the salon atmosphere, but in order for that to happen I had to give myself permission and prepare.

It was during that year I realized how little I knew about the internet and its impact on the future of my career and business. I also realized how far behind the industry was in terms of educating up-and-coming hair professionals on how to keep up with social media business trends.

The hair school I went to is now a rug shop; I'm confident had the owners had this or any other social media strategy book, their business would have survived. They didn't ask for anyone's permission to go out of business, so why should you ask for anyone's permission to STAY in business?

I hope this chapter and the next 22 inspire you to grab control of your own life, behaviour, and destiny and empower yourself to push past those imaginary lines called "peer pressure" and "social acceptance." You're only holding yourself back by not doing so.

The Tipping Point

What set me over the edge was the behaviour of my colleagues and boss while I was studying to improve my client acquisition and marketing skills.

There is something that happens to the human brain when it experiences things like jealousy, fear of loss, or fear of inadequacy. The person who sees you taking massive action starts fighting back with words in the form of snarky remarks. They try to rattle your chain and throw you off with a variety of seemingly plausible comments - everything from "so-and-so did it, and it didn't work" to "that's just not possible."

The individuals in the salon I was at seemed to have no ambition beyond waiting for the weekend to roll around. They would spend their slow times ogling porn, bad-mouthing each other behind their backs, and even sexually harassing each other at times. Sound familiar? I'm well aware this happens at thousands of salons around the country. There's something about our industry.

Most of it was done under the disguise of jokes, but there comes the point in every person's life where sooner or later you're over it. I'm no prude, but when you feel as if enough is enough, something inside you snaps; laughter becomes uncomfortable, and mutual respect for your colleagues turns into resentment.

Be More Selfish, But Do It With Dignity

I arrived at a point in my salon career and the salon I was working at where I felt like I was working alongside a bunch of rowdy teenagers. It didn't feel like I was working with professionals in their 30's and 40's who were supposed to lead by example, some of whom were also parents. I was well aware of the hair culture in my area - I lived it. However, upon discovering Instagram and the early rise of the hair platforms that built a presence on it, I became very interested in connecting with hairstylists myself.

My initial idea was to use social media to connect with hairstylists from all over the world. I wanted to see if I could learn a thing or two from others like me who lived far away and who could offer different perspectives on our industry. I started the process of doing so while I was still working at the salon full time. I had a plan. I was going to have a six month preparation period to arm myself with the information I needed to exit and feel comfortable starting anew.

An interesting thing happened around this time - I started feeling self-empowered. It's a strange feeling, that self-empowerment - it hovers around confidence and "not-giving-a-f***." I liked it and I went on to milk it for all it's worth.

You should do the same.

"You Become the Average of the Five People You Hang Out With"

I was listening to a Tim Ferriss podcast around that time, and although I had never heard of Tim before he said something that stuck with me, and I hope you consider it as well the next time you're observing your work environment. He said that we become the average of the five people we hang out with. That stuck with me. I went to work the next day, and I looked around at everyone's behavior. Like in all broken relationships where people take too much and don't give enough, I realized that the personalities of these humans were toxic and poisonous.

In fact, my awakening to their behavior, the ways it impacted my whole work day, and clouded my creativity really allowed me to evaluate the situation with different lenses. I suddenly decided that such an environment was no longer an ideal place for me to create my dream hair business. They say hindsight is always 20/20, and looking back the only regret I have is not quitting that environment sooner. If this sounds familiar then I suggest a change of environment.

The age of 26 is statistically the age where the most hairstylists quit the salon environment. My number one factor was when I took a good look around and asked myself "is this the kind of environment that I want to spend the rest of my work life in?"

This chapter isn't meant to imply that I'm a better human than anyone else, it's just that I knew I could do a lot better teaching and building businesses with other hair professionals in the industry who may be interested in some of the same things as I am.

In the book Tribes the author Seth Godin talks about how every single person in this world can find their tribe. So through the use of technology and social media communication platforms, I decided to start finding mine. The question is will you find yours?

If you work in a great environment and don't feel the push to make any changes, then perhaps this book will open your mind and allow you to give yourself permission instead of asking others what they think. My intention is to give you a straightforward blueprint and actionable information for finding and retaining more clients using social media tools like Facebook and Instagram. However, you must be aware of the fact that when you start leveling up and wanting more some will try to hold you back.

Humans Sometimes Behave Like Crabs

There is a story called "The Crab In The Bucket" where a handful of crabs were hanging out in the same confined bucket and as soon as one of them would try to climb out to explore the rest of the world, the other crabs would actually pull the escaping crab back down in the bucket with them. What I want you to take away in this chapter and the rest of this book is that whatever your present or your past may be, you don't have to carry it into the future - don't give into the rest of the crabs.

Sometimes all we need is a few good quotes and a different point of view from people who've been we you are to help us start breaking patterns. Small changes can positively impact your life in such a way that you don't feel the need for permission from others every time you do something. You really don't.

The next time you want to make a change in your career, ask yourself one simple question: "is what I'm about to do illegal, immoral, or unethical?" If the answer is no to all three, then start climbing out of your bucket and go take action. What may be immoral is you NOT taking action and changing your circumstance.

Woah Nelly!!!

To clarify, I'm not suggesting that you quit working in a salon altogether. What I'm trying to do is use language as a mechanism to share my experiences so that you feel as if someone else can relate. The truth is, you don't have to start reading books in front of everyone at work, and you don't have to tell anybody what you've got going on. But what I want you to do after you read and apply some of the concepts in this book is to observe the behavior of the people around you.

When you start prospering, whether it's through the flow of more information or more clients, some people around you will enter jealousy mode and what I suggest you do is laugh about it when that happens and don't fight it. When you discover fresh information, you will also be tempted to share with others. Don't.

While your intentions to share the new-found knowledge is to offer help to those around you, often times you being forward with this fresh information may make others feel inferior and defensive. Some will believe you think you're better than them when all you're trying to do is help and spread the good word. Keep it to yourself (for now).

People Pleasing Is Bad Business

If you're a people pleaser like me, you will want to share your experiences with everyone, but as weird as it sounds, most people's attitude will change when they see you do so. They will adopt an air in their attitude that will feel something similar to them saying, "Who are you to tell me what to do?" I want you to be aware of and fully internalize the simple fact that you and you alone are responsible for attracting more clients, making more money, and paying the bills. This is why I recommend you don't share your new knowledge with anyone. Focus your energy on applying it for yourself first.

You must be willing to understand that the fear of the unknown is just that and nothing more. When you go around asking others for permission, their advice usually comes from their fear mechanism regardless of how much you think they want the best for you. If you don't give yourself permission, who will? The person holding you back? Will they?

CHAPTER 2

Finding Gratitude in Technology

Business in general has changed more dramatically over the last 10 years than the 10 years before that. Blame technology and the speed at which information is moving.

Only a few years ago everyone seemed to want to work exclusively with cash, and today if you're paying with cash people think you're old school like, "Who uses cash anymore?" (But I guess it all depends on what part of the world you live in). Yes computers were around, and we used cell phones instead of pagers, but we were using them very differently and not as if they were a part-time job the way we use them today. In the past, you either called someone from your cell phone, or you were running to a phone booth to make a call because you got paged.

Remember the Beeper?

Looking back just 10 years, people mainly used their computers for typing, printing, and searching for information on the odd subject here and there. Now the miniature version of the laptop, the smartphone, is the computer and it weighs half a pound. In fact, I think beepers used to weigh almost as much, and they did almost nothing compared to phones today.

Today's technology is a blessing to small businesses like hair salons and self-employed hairstylists because it provides us with automatic and systematic assistance. Where it was hard to generate a clientele out of thin-air when there was no social media and all you had was tv, radio, and flyer ads to work with, today self-marketing has been made possible for everyone.

Social media has efficiently fixed all the problems of local communication by helping you turn neighbours you haven't met yet into a network (something I'll go in depth on later). With micro-communities like Hairstylist Tribe, you can't help but see the coming technological landscape changes. There is a common way to deal with it, which is to freak out and panic about how fast everything changes. The second is you can give a little thanks and gratitude out into the Universe to the people and companies that create these tools - and that is all they are, tools. When you take three minutes out of your day to feel grateful about how much easier it is to communicate, grow, share, and ultimately prosper using these tools, you'll naturally panic less and less over time.

Forget how far we've come in 10 years - this morning we found my old iPhone 4 from 2014. Three years ago I wasn't able to do anywhere near as many things on Facebook and Instagram that I can do with my one-year-old Samsung S7 Edge. The physical technology had to catch up with how quickly and how much people expected online apps to work for them. They finally did and I am super grateful for today's tech!

CHAPTER 3

The Online Client Relationship Trifecta

Content, Community, and Continuity

One of the reasons people in all sorts of industries fail at attracting and retaining their ideal clients is that they don't know about or understand the simple formula I'm about to describe in this chapter. In later chapters, I will show you practical methods for finding and keeping clients using social media. You will be able to look at those useful methods from a bird's eye view and understand why you can't slack.

Regardless of what specific methods you already follow, the three pillar formulas in the next few pages will help you organize your thoughts by putting all the pieces in the right place. You should also know something I learned the hard way when I first started Hairstylist Tribe - you can't cut corners.

You must be able to follow these three pillars religiously. 1 or 2 won't work on their own without the other two

Community

Whether you're starting a new salon or a new Instagram page, it's safe to assume that you need people's attention in order for them to become clients or followers. This happens through creating a specific community that draws people in.

Community refers to the "feeling" of your online brand when your presence begins attracting attention. In other words, once you find at least one other person who shares your views, you have the beginnings of a community, a tribe. If you're familiar with my online platform, Hairstylist Tribe, you'll know that the community is built around the idea of helping hairstylists and other beauty professionals thrive in social media.

You may be a hairstylist or cosmetologist looking to find and keep more clients. You may also be an industry educator seeking to teach others who are where you once were. Whoever your audience may be, you have to treat them like one of your own. They are the ones who help your business and bank account grow.

Content

This is the pillar that everyone struggles with the most. We're constantly bombarded with "Create Your Own Online Course" and "Be a Woman-preneur Boss Babe" ads, but what a lot of these information peddlers fail to realize when they slap a $3,000 price tag on their course, is that people don't know the fundamentals of content creation, so they have a hard time with advanced courses that are marketed to look easy.

Overpriced information aside, free information can be beneficial when contextualized and offered to a local audience. You see, content creation doesn't necessarily mean you need to teach clients how to do their own hair or be an expert on product use. The kind of content I'm referring to is similar to journaling.

To create this content, you want to record your thoughts on any subject that relates to the beauty industry if you think it will also resonate with your clients. As I'm writing this book, there is a huge separation between what hairstylists do to attract clients and the reality of what the clients are going to respond to. I advise every one of you to give away your knowledge to clients because your words are actually what position you as a person of authority, a professional, and someone who knows what they are talking about in any potential clients' eyes.

The more you hoard your knowledge, the more you will start seeing others have customer success with giving their's away. Distributing content regularly is important to sustaining your growing community. Attention fades fast and 15 minutes of fame has become more like 15 seconds.

Continuity

The third non-optional pillar for keeping your community happy, even if you think you are the greatest content maker of all time, is consistency. In all fairness, this is something I too struggled with when I launched Hairstylist Tribe back in 2014.

I learned a valuable lesson when the community started growing, and the content was outlandish in a way that rubbed some people the wrong way. Sticking with it allowed me to develop grit and evolve my ability to push through during times where I didn't feel like I could.

This pillar is tricky because there is no set number of pieces of content that you have to release online for you to be successful. It can happen after one post or 1,000. This means that you must be patient in order to grow your audience with the content you put out on a continuing bases.

Learn All Three, Do All Three.

These three pillars are the bare bone essentials required to grow your business using social media. It was my objective with this chapter to expose you to the basic foundation of what to do and why in order to have a working formula that will help you gain and keep your momentum. To get started and to keep on moving, it's important for you to know how to apply the foundations to your personal strategy, so you can have a chance to add your flavor the more comfortable you become with the actual work.

There is a lot more that can be said for these topics and the Internet is rife with details and information, but somehow the basics seem unsexy and uninteresting even though they matter the most. Look at it this way; you wouldn't want to learn how to drive on a Lamborghini no matter how attractive the car might be. You would want to learn the basics of driving in a car you can handle. Much in the same way, I want you to be obsessed with the basics because your brain is a wonderful thing and it will let you know when you're ready to take on more.

CHAPTER 4

The Psychology of Social
Media Attention:
Why Salon Clients Do
What They Do Online

Freedom of information is the name of the game and has been for as long as the internet has been around. The only difference between now and a few years ago, is we have access to a lot more information today. The billions of people that own a social media profiles have become increasingly more informed in matters of health, beauty, and personal hygiene. The billions of women connected to the Internet are becoming educated on everything from techniques to the latest hair trends. Clients and potential clients are getting smarter by the day.

It's the summer of 2017 as I'm writing this chapter and social media has been around for a good eight years now; yet, we are still debating the value of social media advertising and marketing. My concern, which I often rant about to our online community, is that we understand *why* clients and future clients do what they do on social media, but as professionals we oftentimes choose to stick to our old ways and not adapt.

In business, potential clients are referred to as leads, people that you need to convince somewhere along the way in your marketing and advertising efforts to book an appointment with you. They are humans like you and me - they are not just a number - and even though this should go without saying, sometimes we forget, through no fault of our own, that humans are behind the social media profiles we interact with.

When you take a moment to quickly remind yourself there is a human on the other end, you tend to have more empathy. When you start thinking like a client, you start opening your mind to all of the opportunities to market yourself because you are thinking like a client, not a hairstylist. You must remember that humans are on the other end of social media accounts if you want your business to survive the social media wave. We must all adapt as we go and be willing to change our perspectives in order to understand how clients want to be marketed to.

Up until the birth of social media, the marketing and business education the beauty industry had access to was lacking. Now that millions of hairstylists are connecting with one another all over the world using their phones, we are rapidly becoming connected to different ways of running our salon businesses, whereas before we were limited to our local hair cultures' ways of doing things. Up until now, beauty professionals hadn't been armed with any actionable advice or education beyond some basic discount techniques up (if you are reading this and disagree with me then you must have been one of the lucky ones).

Facebook and Behavioural Economics

Social media has created a new kind of behavior among shoppers and potential clients. Facebook was built with the reasoning that it would bring the world closer together, but all it did in my opinion was confuse people and make them uneasy about their futures. It was to be expected that when an internet website garnered and kept the attention of million of people it would have an impact on millions of psyches, and not all individuals would react positively to all of this change.

Facebook became what it is today because of the people who started it. Mark Zuckerberg understands the psychology behind people's behaviour at scale, so he created Facebook based on the theory of behavioral economics.

According to the almighty Wikipedia, behavioral economics "is the effects of psychological, and social, cognitive, and emotional factors on the economic decisions of individuals and institutions and the consequences for market prices, and the impact of different kinds of behaviors in different environments. **The study of behavioral economic includes how market decisions are made and the mechanisms that drive public choice.**"

That's a Mouthful!

Zuckerberg created a platform where he knew commerce would happen once many people gathered on it. The astonishing thing about Facebook is that almost everybody I know is active on Facebook. The longer someone uses the platform the platform becomes a part of their daily routine, which often involves shopping around for services and products. Users daily spend an average of two hours on Facebook and check their Instagram 30 times, and it's not limited to seeing what their high school buddies are up to. Facebook has become the digital extension of our personal lives and personalities, the story we tell others about ourselves. The more time people spend on social media, the more likely it is that they will buy.

Although he didn't start Facebook, Steve Jobs is the one we can look at to blame. Zuckerberg would have had a much harder time had Apple not invented the almighty iPhone. Facebook essentially rode the smart phone wave and found ways to become all three of the most used apps: Facebook, WhatsApp, and Instagram, in that order.

Asking WHY will help you identify ways to use social media to your advantage. The HOW is easy. It's the WHY that requires us to step back and look at the bigger picture. Behavioural economics isn't something that many think about or were taught in school, but it is the only theory that fully explains why people do what they do in reaction to where their attention and focus directs. Facebook figured out a way to harness and catch all of that attention better than any other company before.

Everyone thinks Instagram is for the purpose of showcasing ourselves in a better light, and that is true to an extent. But what Facebook and Instagram really are is they are communication vehicles through which we represent ourselves to whomever we are trying to reach. And they're not the only ones. They just happened to be the best ones right now to communicate with almost everyone in your area, whether you know them or not. They also represent the greatest opportunity to grow your business clientele.

If 2 billion people on this planet spend waking moments every day on Facebook, it means Facebook absorbs a lot of attention. The best way to imagine Facebook is as an open wide field with people roaming around in the digital world, and you interact with their phones through the social media platforms. Online everyone is somebody. And there are no strangers, only neighbours you haven't met yet. It's a digital party, and because almost everyone from the real world has come onto the Facebook world, you're job as a hairstylist finding local clients has become exponentially easier than before social media existed.

I remember wondering as a child if there was a way for everyone in the world to be in the same space and communicate all at once. Only 20 years have passed and we now have multiple platforms that allow us to find billions of other people. We may not be connected physically in the real world, but the internet connects each and every one of us in the virtual world. Anyone with a Facebook app is a walking beacon constantly identifying themselves, their location, and their preferences back to Facebook. When you're in a city where almost everyone has a Facebook account, can you see how the power of digital communication combined with that half pound device you call a smartphone can place you in front of potential local clients? Do you see how first identifying yourself as a hairstylist on your Instagram profile, then proceeding to hunt local hashtags on Instagram can help you get more clients? Why does this happen? It's all about attention.

We Live in the Attention Economy!

If the internet was planet earth, then Facebook is the most populated and fastest growing continent on the internet. Every Facebook profile has a digital footprint that it leaves everywhere you go online. When you're dealing with hundreds of millions of users all tapped in and using the same platform, you're effectively staring at the beginning of a digital gold rush where attention is the gold and everyone is rushing to become known in their local area. One of my favorite quotes from Gary Vaynerchuk is, "Before you can sell me or tell me how good your product is, you have to get my attention."

This theory may seem a little provocative, but in the end what I'm trying to convey, is that we as beauty professionals and artists have a tendency to jump the gun and act like we have to be acknowledged just because we made a few hundred posts. I see it time and time again, and it worries me. People give up on finding more clients and better success with their social media efforts because they don't see results right away. I will tell you a simple fact - you're not going to see better results from tv, radio or fliers. Facebook is such an attention monster that you either join it, or you lose out.

Do you know why Donald Trump became President in 2016? It's because 80% of his marketing budget was dedicated to Facebook. His marketing team understood the weaknesses of tv and the strength of Facebook. We used to complain about kids spending too much time watching television, but now Trump became President because he understood 200 million voting Republicans were spending a lot more time on Facebook then watching tv.

At What Point Do We Stop and Ask: Why Is this Important to Know?

Attention is a finicky thing. It's a double edged sword in a sense that once you attain it you then have to keep it. Everyone I know hopes one day a viral video will be made about their life - but really that's just a new way of saying that we want our 15 minutes of fame. Getting attention and keeping attention can get you some online fame, but the question is: what are you going to do with it?

Attention is a fleeting thing - it's constantly getting away from you because the people who have granted you that attention have now moved on, so you have to be willing to create a system to keep it coming back. I'm not immune to it and neither and you. Your clients and potential clients are constantly being bombarded with marketing in every form by your competition directly or indirectly. The truth is, they are one decision away from either choosing you or choosing someone else because of this phenomenon called social media. They may be good people, but for all kinds of reasons including "wanting something knew" hairstylists get cheated on a lot by all sorts of clients.

I suggest that instead of being swept up by this social media wave by not taking control of your attention marketing strategy, you ride the wave by flowing with it and not bucking the current.

Remember that before you can sell somebody something you must first get their attention. The easiest way to do so, before you start any content publishing, is to just take a deep breath and accept what it is.

By this point, you should now feel sufficiently informed on why social media is beneficial from an economic perspective. I often talk about self-empowerment and control, and I want you to know that there are ways to get swept up and controlled by social media, and there are ways that can save you a ton of headaches down the road. The rest of this book focuses on the actions and steps you can take once you're ready to get started.

So let's get to it!

CHAPTER 5

How to Add Value in Today's Social Media Sh*tstorm of Noise and Information

"Clients don't care if you're popular on Instagram, they care about what you can do for them." - Unknown

Keep It Easy, Keep It Simple

As I thought about how I was going to frame this chapter, a little sentence kept nagging me in the back of my head: tell the truth. Popularity doesn't come easy to people telling the truth all the time. However, this truth is harmless to your well-being and can make or break your social media experience.

From my interactions with countless hair pros over the last three years, I've honed my ability to observe and speak to the collective actions of our industry and extract some facts worth writing about. I remain true to the promise I made to myself back in 2014 to only release content when I believed it was ready to be said. There was a second part to that promise - if I was going to say something, it was going to get people to think and it was going to add value.

I secretly asked myself, "What if publishing my opinion to to the hair community mirrors what they already thought, at least some of them? What if it was all it took for them to take action and commit to better behavior in the online digital space?" After over 10,000 messages and countless conversations started, here are a couple of insights into what I've noticed about our industry's behavior on social media, primarily on Instagram.

The Problem + The Solution

The Problem: You tend to care too much about what the popular/celebrity hairstylists do on social media.

I would be lying to you if I told you that I was one of the popular girls in high school. Beating out the boys and winning the Athlete of the Year award didn't help either. Outside of competition, in my social interactions, I tried to be a friend to everyone, but it's only when you mature that you realize if you cater to everybody you just end up pissing off everybody - ya just can't be a people pleaser.

If you're not convinced yet, let's talk statistics. Facebook's internal numbers reveal that the average Facebook and Instagram user spends 3 hours a day looking at social media accounts. Yes, that includes your clients or potential clients in your city as well. During the hours that I spend messaging or responding to requests, I notice the same thing over and over - hairstylists are way too OVER focused on what celebrity hairstylists are doing and posting and UNDER focused on their own desires. If you desire a better Instagram account or larger Facebook audience, then think about who you can serve the best. Here's a hint: It's not other hairstylists. It's the people in your chair (or the people who COULD be sitting in your chair for the first time if you paid attention to them and where they're hanging out)

I find a lot of my conversations end up being me gently talking the other person down off some I've-had-enough-of-social-media mental ledge after they've (supposedly) tried everything. They tried doing what so-and-so does, and it didn't work out. So I have to say, from personal observation...

I'm concerned with the amount of time that our industry spends inflating each other's ego's like it's a high school popularity contest, hoping the popular people on the other end will somehow magically become their best friend and win life for them. It sends a bad message to the fresh-out-of-beauty-school student late teens, early 20s crowd. It intimidates the newbies coming into our industry and gives them the false notion that the big popular accounts are going to grow their skill level somehow, their craft, their marketing, their sales, their customer retention, or somehow magically pay their bills. Please understand that not the President, not your boss, not the celebrity hairstylist you're trying to be friends with, none of these people can have the kind of impact that only YOU can have on YOUR own life.

So what should you do to step away from that constant urge of needing validation from others and wanting to feel popular on Instagram? What do you do if you want to build a base of attentive followers? Start by finding ways to add value. Tell people what you've learned throughout the day - document it. Connect with the millions of clients all over Instagram and Facebook. Document your journey as you grow whether you blog or record video. Sell us more on who you are, what you overcame, what you've learned...and stop trying to sell us on your MLM schemes and classes.

It's incredible how many people pander to the weaknesses and insecurities of hair professionals by making them believe they need that extra class, or that extra product to sell, or that extra trip somewhere away from their family for the weekend.

You know what you need?

You need to do you more.

Put yourself on the pedestal instead of others.

Be slightly more selfish - just a tad.

Start by caring more about yourself, your wallet and your family. Think about it logically. Not I, not the other hairstylists you follow, pay the bills. You do. It's up to you to educate yourself and grow and learn but how many mingling and mixing and classes can you go to? How many social accounts can you follow for inspiration?

There isn't anything you need to focus on right now except finding more clients so you can start charging more so you can start earning more.

HERE'S WHAT YOU DO:

To start, take an hour out of the two or three you spend on your phone each day to look in on what's happening in your area by tuning in to hashtags. Find hashtags specific to your city (it probably has thousands or millions) and start by liking and commenting on local people's photos.

I mean REALLY engage with them, don't install an Instagram robot.

When they see your comment, they naturally go and take a look at your hair page. They're now aware of you. You don't have to sell them right away; they just have to know you're there to start off with. Spend those two or three hours creeping potential clients accounts instead of other stylists' accounts. There is only so much masterminding, conferencing, cruising, mixing, mingling, introducing, networking, connecting, and traveling to classes one can do. Stop and realize just how precious your time is.

Our industry is finally on the cusp of having our services being sought after through emerging digital platforms like Instagram and Facebook. Please understand that not all industries have the ability for a client to turn on a phone, look at photos, and hit the "Call Now" button for an appointment. Don't take Instagram and Facebook for granted - take advantage of their existence instead. Observe the industry from a new vantage point and then run some Facebook ads. Boost your post. Tell your city/town who you are and what you're all about — show them what you can do, show them your portfolio.

I know people in other industries, like painters, who can invest hundreds of dollars on Facebook or Instagram ads but will never get a call because people aren't used to finding painters on Facebook. Clients are used to finding hairstylists on Instagram and Facebook.

Other hairstylists aren't your target market - stop paying attention to them. Start paying attention to people who could be paying your bills. Be yourself, start teaching future clients about our industry instead of rubbernecking with other hair professionals in forums and at conferences.

"Be the change you want to see in the world - even if it's only in the beauty world." - Unknown

Consider adopting a position of opinion on any subject in our industry you feel strongly about, especially one where people may either agree or strongly disagree with your views. This is a branding move that acts as an anchor which will become one of the many principles you build your online personality and business around. It's a fundamental principle, not a tactic or strategy, which people can tie to your online persona - branding starts with adding value in order to become recognizable in the midst of all the noise. That's how you start really marketing and advertising your services, by being recognizable as the go-to hair shaman with all the answers.

So go, answer your followers' questions on hair, and stand out from the crowd - be the local hairstylist people aren't afraid of reaching out to and connecting with.

CHAPTER 6

Follow Your DNA

If you can't tell by now, I'm a huge fan of consumer psychology. Not the mind control and manipulative type of psychology; I'm talking about understanding consumer behavior and what businesses do to better serve them in the places where they spend most of their time. Throughout my research for this book, I've studied a large number of people in our industry in order to understand them better and, quite frankly, because I wanted to see what they are all about. Most of these people - not all, but the vast majority of them - posture and hold themselves up to be social media experts.

The funny thing is though, none of them speak to the main problem professionals face, which is the lack of content creators in our industry. Most of them offer blanket solutions based on what they've learned, but it always seems to be a band-aid solution for the hairstylist, not actionable advice someone can run with. What these social media experts don't realize is that there are three mediums of communication available to humans: video, written word, and audio.

Humans enjoy various digital content delivery methods such as Netflix and YouTube. So if you hop on the latest trend bandwagon, which currently is live video, you might be doing yourself a disservice, because video is not where you may be the strongest. At the time I'm writing this book, audio experiences are exploding in popularity, and our industry, being so visual, hasn't fully adopted the podcasting trend (yet).

Are you going to be the one who changes the status quo? I'm certain you can if you follow your DNA.

We are constantly bombarded with reasons why we should do video over podcasts, but the trend of the general market doesn't care about your individual preferences. The goal of the platform market is to get you to consume what's easiest for you to consume, but that doesn't mean you are a creator of the kind of content that the market is looking for. Likewise, your strengths may lie in doing recorded and edited videos instead of live video. They may lie in your ability to have a radio voice, where you feel much more comfortable speaking than writing or being in front of a camera.

Bonus, when you follow your own guidance and start going in the direction of what you feel comfortable with, you won't burn out as fast. That's the advantage to following your DNA.

Once you recognize that humans can communicate to the masses by writing, audio, and video, you have the ability to try all three before you commit to any one way, no risk involved. I ask that you consider each one and take some time (two to three months) before you decide if any one way is the right strategy for you. Maybe multiple strategies will work best. You won't know unless you try a bunch of times. In other words, you must communicate to your audience in a way where you feel comfortable because that's when you become better, it's when your mind opens, and it's when you will actually thrive in getting your message out to your audience of current and future clients.

I'm personally a huge fan of writing because time is precious and I don't want to waste my audience's attention by doing live streaming. I like to get straight to the point because there are a lot of moving parts that get social media to work in your favour and I value my time as much as I value my audience's. I share my thoughts more in writing than I do on video; I follow my DNA.

However...

It doesn't mean that your photography skills are outdated just because video streaming is popular, and it doesn't mean people will stop listening to audio experiences. In fact, podcasting and voice skills are currently the fastest growing trend in content creation and distribution. While it is true that it is easier to get more attention on a video than blogs and podcasts, we also live in a time where people are becoming increasingly open to the idea of consuming various types of content for many reasons, primarily, to save time.

Audio is the new live video. Although I personally enjoy writing, I would highly recommend that you consider giving podcasts/audio recordings a shot. We are flooded with videos everywhere we go, but the fact is that audio experiences require only one level of sensory focus and are therefore easier to consume while multitasking. In my opinion, video will completely dominate in a few decades when every car drives itself, but right now commuting is actually the reason why audio experiences are shooting up in popularity. It's just easier to listen and drive than to watch a video and pay attention to the road at the same time.

Remember the Napster trend in the early 2000's, when music was being downloaded and consumed more than any other media? You might notice now in 2017 that music has been commoditized to the point people that want more than entertainment coming in on their speakers - they want knowledge.

When the internet was young, internet connections were slow, and podcasts were not a thing yet, the only practical use anyone got out of audio experiences was entertainment/escapism. Now that our phones have become our main source of information and replaced the bulky home computers (and in some cases even replaced the television), we are all collectively seeing that this half-pound device called the Smartphone has so many more uses than just entertainment.

Final Point

Don't be afraid of doing the thing that is opposite of what everyone is doing. If you're shy like me, then podcasting or writing is a great alternative to constantly having your face on camera. You may have heard the phrase "she has a radio voice, " and you just may be one of the people that has a radio voice. We often mistake the type of medium we enjoy consuming for it being the same medium we should create content in, but that's just not true.

For example, I prefer watching the HBO series Game Of Thrones over reading the book series, but it doesn't mean that's where my strengths lie when it's time for me to create content.

The other major confusion that is very common in our industry is looking at someone who does well on camera and thinking that's what we're supposed to replicate. It just isn't so. It's best if you follow your intuition and create content for the medium that you feel most comfortable with, even if it's the one that is the current flavour of the month.

After all, it is the message that matters, not the medium.

CHAPTER 7

When to Post, What to Post, and How Direct Messaging Builds Your Ideal Brand

I had mixed feelings about writing a chapter on the timing of posts, but as I thought about it I remembered that even though Instagram has been around for over seven years, this topic is still a sticking point for many in our industry. While assembling of the chapter outline for this book, I wanted to use this popular question to explain the answer once and for all, and to shift the focus towards something that will have a much larger impact on your brand's growth than just getting the perfect timing down pat. My goal with this chapter is to shift our industry's attention from unimportant minutiae to the questions that will allow you to grow your business in a practical way.

So to answer this question of when to post once and for all, in short, IT DOESN'T MATTER! You just have to do it, and do it daily.

There are two questions that are of grave importance that one should ask themselves if they are trying to build a local social media following of potential local clients:

1. What do I post?

2. How do I engage with people who like, comment, or follow my profile?

What Do I Post?

I will not go into the specifics of how to take and edit photos because I already assume that you own a smartphone or iPad. If you've made it this far, I would assume that you already have your own way in creating the content that best showcases your talents and skills. Chances are that you have a phone with a good camera, and to be quite frank, average quality phone pictures do a lot better on Instagram and Facebook than overly polished editorial photos. I don't make the rules; I just report on the facts as I experience them.

The biggest problem hairstylists face when posting is overthinking and over-analyzing strategies until the brain becomes overwhelmed, and they end up feeling not worthy of posting at all. They psyche themselves out. There is no perfect way to post, and if you're just starting out, you're going to naturally improve over time.

See for Yourself

If you're still unconvinced, I would suggest checking out the Hairstylist Tribe Instagram feed from the very beginning. The one-hundredth post on our profile was a much better post than the first, but definitely not as good as the one-thousandth post. It's not very sexy to tell people not to overthink their posts which is why many hair marketing experts don't talk about it. It's much sexier for you to be sold on a secret complicated formula then a simple one. The trick is to just do before you have a chance to overthink. It's much more important to make imperfect content posts and adjust over time.

Of course you have to be aware of things such as lighting and angles, but those are cheap and easy fixes that aren't necessarily the point of your feed. The biggest thing you should think about is to remember to take photos and videos more often. The real challenge is remembering to take before and after photos of all of your clients; it's a habit that will take you about two months to actually make part of your daily work routine.

I hope that you have enough patience and faith in yourself to make imperfect posts and improve as you go and as you discover new ideas.

Why Your Photos Aren't Showcased

There are two reasons most hairstylists who submit hair transformation photos don't get featured on Hairstylist Tribe. I'm confident that once you fix these two things, your content stream will look a lot cleaner and presentable.

Reason #1: Taking a photo too close to the client's hair.

When you stand too close to your client, a few things happen. First, the crown of the head gets cut off. The reason this trend continues to happen is that the large hair profiles either don't care or don't understand photography aesthetics. Second, the moment you are too close, the photo on Instagram turns out blotchy. It doesn't show the whole head, and often the photo looks like it's showcasing hair fibers instead of an artist's actual finished work. What potential clients want to see in every post they look at is 1) the satisfied expression on your client's face and 2) the way their hair looks overall, not just a patch of hair.

The solution is simple - next time you take a photo, notice how closely you normally stand to your clients and take one normal step back. The photo or video will look a lot more professional when you showcase the entire finished look, whether it's from the side, front, or back of the head.

Reason #2: Having more than two images in the same photo.

I also made this mistake when I first launched Hairstylist Tribe, thinking that more is better. It's not. Actually, less is more. You wouldn't want to have two videos side by side, so why bother having two or three photos side by side? Here's a hot tip about collage photos - since you are willing to take multiple photos to create one collage image, why not consider posting each one of those photos separately?

What this does is twofold. It gives you more content to post over time from just one client, and it also makes your profile look a lot cleaner. Just because Instagram allows multiple images in the same photo, it doesn't mean it will be appealing to the eye. To make matters worse, the more photos you use in one post, the less you'll have to post as content.

How Do I Engage With People Who Like, Comment, and Follow My Profile?

This is a newly popular feature that has been around for a couple of years. However, it's still underused. Instagram was such a new concept, and what with the posts, likes, and comments features, everyone seemed to forget that this platform is really a chat platform first and a photo platform second. We got so used to the idea of posting photos with hashtags that we forget to actually use this basic feature to converse with the humans that validate our posts with comments and hearts in the first place!

Get familiar with direct messaging, it's the #1 social media tool you should be using to connect with local clients. DMing is so underused that if you start simply messaging your followers to thank them for paying attention to your profile, you will instantly become memorable. They will be pleasantly surprised, and those 25 seconds each you spend messaging followers may be the difference between a client coming to you or going to someone else. I've messaged every single one of the people that follow Hairstylist Tribe over the last three years, and thousands of them had the same response: "I'm shocked there is a human behind this profile and that you took the time to message me!" The reason why everyone is so shocked is that no one else does it.

There are a lot of hair accounts on Instagram that are run by multiple people, sometimes as many as ten folks have their hands in at a time, and none of them take the initiative to message their followers. Where you have the advantage of making an impact and leaving a lasting impression is by going deep with the few followers you have instead of trying to go wide to pad your follower numbers. You may not have ten people helping you, but you also only have a few hundred or thousand followers. It's crucial that you do your best to stand out from the other hairstylists in your area. Large hair accounts are slow to adapt, and you as a one-person show are nimble, quick, especially because you only have yourself to consult. You don't have lots of other personalities to deal with; it's just you and the person you are trying to forge a relationship with. This is your biggest advantage - you can pivot often.

Of course I don't make a secret of the fact that my welcome messages to followers are partly scripted. Just as you might copy and paste confirmation messages to clients, I pre-script part of the message, but I am always the one sending it. Most importantly, I always address the person by their name and include appropriate emojis. I do this because a robot will not do it, so the person automatically knows I'm a real human behind the account.

What Do I Do After They Respond?

I suggest you respond to the person's message when they get back to you. This will allow you to show your followers that you're not only willing to break the ice and say hello, but that you're willing to engage with them long term. I encourage you to practice shifting your mindset and behavior from the "popularity" mindset that large hair accounts are known for and start showing your followers how much you care about their hair health. Adding value through proactive communication is just as important as showcasing your services. There are hundreds of different ways you can do to build your brand, but this is a free and effective way to ensure that you are memorable.

Only you know your schedule and your lifestyle, but the 30 seconds that you invest in messaging a stranger who wants to follow your work may reward you with a long term client and a friend. Please find your ideal amount of time that you're willing to put into your business outside of salon hours. Consider examining the hours in the day where you're sitting around doing things that don't benefit you; instead of checking Snapchat for the twentieth time, whip out your phone, set up a 15-minute timer, and message away.

The may seem tedious, but what will keep you going is when some of those people starting messaging you back to say thank you. At this point, you are seen as a hair professional who cares about the client's time, and this simple gesture will compound. Any amount of time you can dedicate is worth it - the work you put in on your social media accounts will eventually be directly reflected in the amount of business you see coming into your chair. It will stack up on itself, and you will have a much better chance of turning followers into clients.

The time you invest in social media interaction yields best results when you pay attention to detail and add your own personal touch in every communication you have. Because of the anonymity of social media, clients and future clients value one on one time much more than ever before.

Overthink Less, Document More!

So stop worrying overmuch about timing your posts and instead work on creating habits around properly documenting your work and posting that content daily. This shows potential clients whom you've recently engaged with that you're busy, sought after, and have a steady flow of clientele which acts as social proof to prop you up.

CHAPTER 8

Turning Followers Into Clients: The Power of Local Hashtags

Now that you understand the power of direct messaging, you will have more confidence to start and continue conversations with the intention of building relationships that will have a chance later on to turn followers into paying clients. Once you feel comfortable with DMs, you will want to ramp up your efforts so that you can have a proper long-term branding strategy. This chapter focuses on how to add specificity to your brand's growth. I'm going to explain why most hairstylists unknowingly use the wrong hashtags and how to use the right ones to grow your social media presence freely.

The following advice assumes that you're in the majority of hairstylists who don't travel for work, you would like to build your clientele, and that you want those clients to be within driving distance of your business.

The Power of Local Hashtags

The number one mistake that every service professional, including hairstylists, makes is that they use popular, well known, big brand hashtags. This is a mistake. The reason this is a mistake is that the average client looking for a salon doesn't search the hashtags of big brands we hair professionals are familiar with.

Put yourself in the shoes of a client and consider the types of hashtags a client would use or pay attention to in order to find a hairstylist in their area. Now think about it from your own perspective. Do you want to spend all your time engaging with people hundreds of miles away from your salon? You probably want to concentrate your efforts on followers in your area who are more likely to become clients. You will be much more effective if you focus your efforts on local hashtags.

Frankly, clients don't care about big brands' hashtags - only stylists do and other stylists aren't exactly your target audience. Clients care about finding a stylist that they can reach within a reasonable drive. The way they find those stylists and the way you can find those clients is by focusing on hashtags that are proprietary to your area and the town or city you live in. Because there's really no point in using brand hashtags that clients won't search for when you can use hashtags of local sports teams, events, venues, or local attractions.

What Do You Think Is Better?

A hashtag used by only hair professionals or a hashtag that was used by a local citizen that you now have the advantage of engaging with on their own posts? The exciting thing about local hashtags is that you have the opportunity to take full advantage of the thousands of posts that are hashtagged in your city by starting conversations with people that live within driving distance of your business. Liking and or commenting on local posts are wonderful ways to help people become aware of you and your work.

Now, this only works if you are not being pushy or annoying them with services and discounts off the bat. Don't do that; be patient. You absolutely must be able to shut out the monkey part of your brain that wants to pitch everything to everybody. Be cool about it - spend time getting to know your potential clients, follow their accounts, send them messages, tell them how awesome their posts are, and let things play out.

Clients are smart, and the restraint you have in pitching your services, the more likely they are going to pay attention to you long term. When you act in a way that is too transactional, you give potential clients the impression that you are desperate and that is a big turn off.

Do What Others Are Unwilling To Do

In our fast-paced, social media-driven world where the average attention span is eight seconds for a video and only four seconds for a photo, we all must increase our efforts to keep potential clients paying attention to our work. After all, there are plenty of fish in the sea of hairstylists for clients to choose from.

The reason I chose to write a book was because I wanted to be competitive with other beauty industry marketing professionals. Writing a book was the natural progression for me to stand above the crowd. The reason you are reading this book is I somehow convinced you, at some point, that my advice is good for you. So imagine what can happen if you take this concept, apply it to your business, and do something similar for potential clients that others are either unwilling to do for them (or maybe just don't know how).

You have the advantage of knowledge, and as long as you take consistent action and use that knowledge to constantly connect with new people, you will always have an advantage over every other beauty professional that doesn't put in the work.

"But Melissa, If It Were So Easy Everyone Would Do It!"

Fair question, but don't let that attitude be a cop out. The fact us that only about 1% of individuals try at least once. So if you live in a large city like L.A. or New York where there are thousands of stylists, 1% of 1,000 for example, is 10. That means only 10 people out of every 1,000 who consume information or advice that they know is good for them will take action. I don't know about you, but with that statistic in mind I get a rush knowing that the most important strategy of all is just simply to do it.

In a city like Los Angeles where millions of people live, about half of those are women, and at least half of those women are are always looking for a better hairstylist. If you happen to be one of the ten people who takes consistent action, doesn't give up when it doesn't work right away, and continues to follow the plan I have suggested, you will see results. It doesn't take rocket scientist to understand that in our information-bombarded world, people are seeking attention on an ongoing basis. This means it's only a matter of time before local hashtagers turn into followers, and from followers into clients.

Top-of-the-Mind or Bust!

Social media gives you the ability to remain at the top of the potential client's mind. Once the client is aware of and follows you, your daily posts will start garnering attention from your local followers, and when they need a new hairstylist - guess who they will go to? YOU. As I mentioned previously, if you take 15 to 30 minutes per day to focus specifically on gently letting locals in your area know you exist by "creeping" local hashtag" and engaging with their posts, you will be amazed at the kind of responses you will receive.

However, the advancements in technology and speed of human communication have created a fake narrative about how fast things should happen for us. When you couple that reality with the sensationalist media, which makes everything seem like it happens overnight, it's no wonder that people get discouraged when a project they take on doesn't work out right away.

Be a Turtle in a Hare's Body

Once you make a decision to act, you have to be quick as a hare and take action before you give yourself a chance to talk yourself out of it. In the same breath, you must also have the patience of a turtle and know you're not going to get to the finish line as fast as you like. It takes time. After all, what goes up quick comes down just as quick. What builds slow, take a much longer time to fall apart.

Distractions, Distractions, Distractions...

I'm fully aware of the types of business and pyramid schemes that all of us are constantly exposed to, where we are somehow mesmerized with words and told that this product or service is going to magically make us rich overnight. The one thing that these multi-level marketing schemes get right every time when they pitch their products to us professionals is they tell us that it's a numbers game. This I agree with.

So make your own numbers game. Do the work and move yourself into a mindset where you care about the potential clients before they even know who you are. Showcase how-to videos or provide some other value on your small-but-thriving profile and as I suggested before. Stop comparing yourself with others'. You have your own path to follow. Out of the thousands of women in your area, you will be one of the few hair professionals that actually stands a chance to turn a followers into clients using nothing but social media and hard work - but first you must stand out and allow future clients to become aware of you and get to know you. And again, it takes time.

CHAPTER 9

Create More Content,
Land More Clients

Up until this point, I have discussed the importance of going where your future audience already hangs out. I have mentioned local hashtags and the ultimate strategy nobody ever teaches in our industry, which is to go where your clients already are as opposed to expecting them to come to you.

I want you now to put aside your ego and your feelings for a second and truly understand how big and populated social media is. I want you to allow the size of it to sink in for a second and lower your expectations about being "found." The more people who join these platforms, the less likely the chance you'll be found through your posts alone. Over the last seven years, we've been taught that hashtagging our posts is enough to be discovered, but now you understand why hashtagging is not enough anymore - you must be proactive and go and find your future followers instead of engaging in "hope marketing" and hoping that they will find you.

I've offered this advice to thousands of hairstylists through my content. The ones that did it, saw results. Now that you know that you have to go out and find followers, I want to return to the part of social media that you're already used to hearing about from other experts.

Content Is King

Content keeps your profile current and the chance of finding local clients that much higher. If you stop posting content, potential clients will think that you've quit or that they won't be able to get reach you via social. So it's important to share everything you take a photo of.

Almost every hairstylist that I have had a private discussion with over the last 3 years, has asked me to judge their social media profile. Although 99% of them were great, at least half of the hairstylists thought their profile was not good enough. Almost every one of them has felt insecure about their social media presence because they did not see any engagement - so they automatically thought it must be because their content is crappy. Nothing can be farther from the truth.

Sometimes it can feel like the few hundred other hairstylists who you perceive as having a nicer profile and more engaged audience are doing something right and you're not. Yes, you are constantly bombarded with others' work, but you have to remember that on social media, similarly to the real world, there are tens of thousands of hairstylists, but there are billions of clients. Let that sink in for a moment. It is only our brain that tricks us into thinking the grass is greener on someone else's profile when in fact, they started with insecurities themselves. They found their way and you must too.

If you go back and look at the first 2 - 300 posts on Hairstylist Tribe Instagram profile, you will see the beginnings of what is now a highly professional profile. However, three years ago it wasn't. You must be willing to accept that where you are now isn't where you're going to be in the future.

Your content may be great, but it's your lack of engagement that is a problem. Chances are you aren't posting enough and not engaging in your local hashtags. You have to do both. The point of this chapter is to help you understand that there are layers of work that you must undertake and habits you must build to actually see the results you want to see. A proper social media profile growth strategy isn't about doing one thing that will work; it's about understanding that it takes several different tactics that make up your long-term strategy.

You must shift your mindset from one of expectation that people will find you tp one of being on the prowl for your future followers and clients. It's almost like sending flyers to people's homes; you must put out "feelers" for you to have a chance of someone knowing you exist in business. While I don't suggest you spend the time and money investing in actual physical flyers, I do want to point out that reaching out using local hashtags on social media is similar to sending flyers in the real world.

People Live on Their Phones

We live in a digital world where you must make people aware of your existence. If you open a physical salon and you never advertise that you're open, you might as well not exist because it takes years for enough people to notice you. What I'm talking about is a strategy where you're proactive. You show potential local clients that you exist, and then when they come check out your "digital location," a.k.a your online portfolio, you have content ready for them. I want you to focus your efforts on steadily creating content posts for your online salon presence while being proactive and going out there into the digital world to make yourself known to local neighbors who may be one day become your friends and clients.

Going back to the idea of doing more than one thing as part of your overall social media growth, you must be willing to continue your daily posts with ZERO expectations of being found. You must put yourself in a position to be found and be aggressive instead of passive. 99% of the hair Instagram profiles I have come across are more than good enough to attract new followers and local clients. The disconnect in most hair professionals' lives is the lack of proactivity. Part of finding, attracting, and keeping an audience is being consistent with your posts. A funny thing happens the more consistent you are: your posts get better and more people start seeing them!

There is no "perfect," and there never will be. We can only aim for "excellent," and it's a lot easier to achieve social media excellence then it is to do hair I can tell you that much. I say this because I've seen thousands of profiles of hairstylists way more talented than me, but still comparing themselves to others who often times didn't do great work but had a nice profile. You to take it upon yourself to build up your social media skills, much in the same way you have built up your hairdressing skills. Think about it - you use chemicals on your client's scalps, you navigate their carotid artery with a sharp scissor, and to top it all off you turn the fiber on their head into art, yet you're insecure about how the photo for your artwork looks and what people think about it? You may be doing fantastic work, but if you lie to yourself and say you don't, you'll hold yourself back from putting it out and finding clients. Not sharing your work with the world hurts your wallet as much as it hurts your self confidence. JUST POST IT!

CHAPTER 10

If You Need New Clients This Week

Welcome to the most important section of this book. It took nine other chapters to build a foundation for the idea I've been trying to build up in your minds. It took some explaining for a simple idea to be understood correctly.

If you are feeling pumped about getting to work and applying some of these concepts, you'll be happy to know that this chapter explains a simple and easy-to-follow the process on how to market your salon services for free. Just keep in mind that when you're not investing dollars, you are investing your time instead. So, I ask before you throw out the excuse of "I don't have time." Do a short self-analysis and figure out in which part of your waking life you can carve out 30 to 60 minutes each day in order for you to market your services properly in the new digital age that we live in.

One of the main hurdles that separates stylists from finding new clients quickly is their preconceived notion that advertising their services is in someway "dirty" or "annoying" to potential clients. Whatever your personal beliefs on advertising and investing dollars into your business, I ask that you park them somewhere in the back of your mind.

This chapter is all about no-cost marketing - a.k.a generating awareness for your brands and services by putting in time and effort to connect with like-minded local people who may need your hair expertise. They are neighbours you haven't met yet. A huge misconception in our industry is the idea that thousands of followers from all over the globe all of a sudden matter to you, the local physical business. They don't, local followers do. As much as you'd like to think globally, you are a local business in a global market. While globalization may matter to a lot of other industries, the truth is, as a hairstylist you deal with local clients, so why not think locally?

When a talented hairstylist who posts great work and has an infinite amount of potential to grow is worried because she doesn't have tens of thousands of followers, it reminds me of an episode from the Netflix series Black Mirror. The setting of the episode "Nose Dive" is a world not too far away from our current social behavior where popularity and availability of rights and choices boil down to how high your personal rating is out of five. If you've been in an Uber or were asked to rate a WhatsApp call, you know what I am talking about. However, in that world, human relationships and interactions regressed down to a social structure where people only cared about the other persons rating and not who they really are.

Although sometimes it may feel like you're living the in Black Mirror universe, you don't need a thousand followers from all over the world in order to feel better about yourself and grow a clientele. What you need is a hundred local followers, out of which ten to twenty become clients, which puts money in your pocket and improves your life.

Enough beating around the bush and avoiding the problem by telling yourself, "But I already hashtag my work!" That's no longer as easy as it used to be. Put aside the idea of thousands of followers. Adding tags to your posts and hoping you will be found via hashtag is very 2010 - it's no longer a reliable strategy. What I suggest you do is continue to share your work, and instead of spending the time worrying about not being found through your hashtags proactively search for others in your local areas popular hashtag.

Stop sitting around hoping you will be discovered. You need to be aggressive with your time. Even if you go no further than this chapter and choose not to push yourself to learn paid advertising and automation, which I talk about later in the book, then I encourage you to at least implement what I suggest in this chapter and do it daily for 60 minutes at a minimum (set a timer). You must spend time in your local hashtag Instagram feed and break the ice by engaging, commenting, and giving kudos to the posts you like seeing. In your local hashtag feed there are thousands of opportunities each day for you to engage with local neighbours you have not yet met.

Powerful Stuff, I Know

Of course, you don't have to like every photo in the news feed this is where your true side shows - you have to actually like the post. Be genuine, even when you're on the prowl for new followers and clients. If you relate to the local post in some way, then engage with it and follow the person who posted it.

Now this is where it gets even better - Instagram has a soft limit on engaging with posts, and after about 50 to 60 engagements, you are no longer able to engage with anyone until the next day. This is your advantage because it only takes 30 to 60 seconds to engage with a post, check out the profile and hit the follow button. It will take you no more than 30 minutes total. The other 30 mins of your social media day should be spent engaging further with the people that followed you back. This is the bread and butter, where the rubber meets the road, and the one-on-one interactions and conversations between you and potential local clients start to happen. There is no parade, no rock music, no fireworks when this happens - it isn't some unattainable thing. You constantly have to remind yourself that if you want local clients, local followers are what matter.

As you receive follow-backs, you will want to dedicate your time to helping these client leads with any hair questions they may have. Some of you may be skeptical about giving your knowledge away for free, but that's all this is, is the exchange of information. Informing your client drives their trust levels up, and you're not just seen as some hairstylist who simply wants to pitch them your services. Clients are smart. They already understand it's implied that you are talking to them because you are hoping to earn their business. They will think it's very creative. So get creative.

Wait!!!

When you start receiving local followers, do not - I repeat DO NOT - sell them on your services right away. Help them first by answering their questions in real time. You spend all day on your phone anyway, so you might as well show potential clients what you know by sending a few valuable messages back and forth. Answer their questions to establish authority and expertise in their minds. The chance of them becoming a client increases exponentially.

How to Engage with New Potential Clients

Sometimes it's the simple things that make the most difference. What I'm about to say sounds simple, but almost nobody does it. If you plan on turning your followers into clients at some point, a direct message once they followed you back is highly recommended. You will want to appear as human as possible when you are interacting with your followers on your hair account. Ensure that the direct message is specific, personal, and engaging.

You don't want your followers to think they are speaking to a robot. It takes 15 to 20 seconds to send out a short welcome and thank you message, and there is a 50 person limit on how many messages you can send per day. So take advantage of it. This is what helps us grow the Hairstylist Tribe attention base over time. I engaged with every one of you as you followed our account, and that went along way. Hairstylist Tribe remained memorable. Your mission should be to be memorable. The way you become that is by doing something others aren't willing to do.

I said it before, and I will say it again - you don't need thousands of followers from all over the world. You need a few hundred followers from your area, some of whom will become hair clients in the future if you just help them first. However, this is where you may or may not become a little bit impatient. When you start interacting with a bunch of your followers, and you realize that all of them are local, you'll be tempted to turn them into clients right away. You will be tempted to tell them all about your great services and your discounts.

Don't Do It!

Immediately trying to sell followers on your services will turn them off. People want to get to know their future hair professionals first; they want to ask questions and be helped by a new hairstylist. So if you want to earn the trust of local followers and turn them into clients, just be patient and help these people before they commit to an appointment. You will see that somewhere between them being your social media followers, and the moment they finally decide to sit in your chair, is a long enough road where a friendship can start between the stylist and the client.

Now you have a roadmap for what you can do on social media with a zero-dollar advertising budget. If after reading all this, you're still looking to grow your business and base of attention even faster then doing it the free way, I suggest you skip this free marketing strategy and move on to the next chapter. Jump straight into paid social media advertising. Do what I call the "$5/day salon marketing budget." If you can afford a $5 daily advertising budget, then I encourage you to start boosting some of your Instagram posts and place them in front of local clients, as I'll show you in the next chapter.

Every chapter from here on out is more advanced and specific. I encourage you to go ahead and implement a plan with everything I laid out in the first ten chapters as you continue to read - you now have everything you need to get started and see results. Good luck!

CHAPTER 11

Pay To Play For a Sustainable Hair Clientele

I want to congratulate you first of all for making it this far! You have moved passed the free marketing strategy I outlined in chapters one through ten. From here on out, almost all of the advice and strategies I outline involve paying to play. While I highly recommend you finish reading this book either way, if you don't have an advertising budget yet, start focusing all your attention on what you have learned so far, and keep the information in the rest of this book as a reference for the future.

Facebook is essentially the keeper and organizer of the attention of the people. Not only does Facebook own large amounts of data, it's also populated by two billion users. Facebook is also the mother company of Instagram, which utilizes Facebook information to help you target your ideal followers. With a marketing budget, you don't pay Facebook to give you clients - you invest in Facebook (which is considered a business expense) in order for Facebook to place your work and offerings in front of your actual future clients. The cherry on top of Facebook being over two billion strong is that it will help you target potential clients locally because everyone around you is on Facebook. Try targeting 1,000 women for $10 on TV or through fliers - it is not possible. We've built an entire community on Instagram and Facebook using nothing but websites and apps.

What Do I Actually DO to Get There?

The quickest way for you to get started and boost your first Facebook or Instagram post is to go into the App or Play Store on your mobile device and search for "Facebook Ads." What you will find is something called "Facebook Adverts Manager" by Facebook, INC. Once you download this app, you will be good to go. At this point, it's important to remember whether or not you turned your Instagram account from a personal profile to a business profile.

Aside from what your personal opinion of social media may be, whether you dislike one or another, you must remember that your wallet doesn't care about your feelings on social media. You'll be able to promote your posts on either Instagram or Facebook, not necessarily both at the same time. Having said that, there are two ways to go about advertising on Instagram or Facebook. In this chapter I'm going to cover the easiest one you can apply today.

Discover Facebook Adverts Manager

Things have changed quickly on Facebook over the last three years, especially over the last two where advertising increased, and the number of marketers quadrupled. Beauty professionals must recognize that no matter how hard we may try to fight the social media current, we are already riding the wave. The goal of this chapter is to give you a soft nudge into the next level of business. First, you must actually see yourself as a business - and as that business, you must be willing to invest in order to grow.

Your idea of being a self-sufficient hairstylist is great, but you must be able to walk the talk, and if you're going to call yourself a business person who generates income from offering hair services, then you need to think like a real business. Real businesses have advertising budgets. The same way I recommend in chapter ten that you find time in your day to do free marketing for your salon services, in this chapter I recommend that you find disposable income from your everyday life in order to fund a $10 daily salon marketing advertising budget. Rest assured that in return Facebook will treat you like a real business and email you receipts for all the investments you've made in the Ads you've boosted on their network.

This is exactly how easy Facebook made it for you, the one-hairstylist show. Through its Ad platform, Facebook allows you access to future local clients by helping you land in their Facebook feeds. As much as you hear about big multinational companies (and Facebook is definitely one of them), I have yet to come across an attention-buying mechanism as great as Facebook Advertising.

You need to ride this wave

In order for you to set up your first advertising post, you will need to understand a handful of the parameters that you will be advertising based off of. Facebook calls them "target demographics." Remember when A/S/L (age, sex, location) was popular? Facebook works much in the same way by allowing you to post your work and target people of all ages in your local area.

If you haven't noticed by now, every time you open your news feed on Facebook, every second or third post in your scroll is a sponsored post. This doesn't stop there. The more you scroll down, the more you realize that the 9th or 12th post is also sponsored. Your advertisements will fit nicely in the feed of local women who are within driving distance of the salon you work at.

To top it all off, Facebook sets you up for further success by allowing you to have your clients and future clients tap through a book now or call now button. It is so easy it's surreal. Listen, you already know everyone and their mother is on Facebook - literally! So start investing in your future now and allow yourself to have a chance to have a long-term client acquisition and retention strategy.

Before you you are able to sell something to clients, you must get their attention first. Facebook is great for a self-employed hair professional, as well as a salon owner's saving grace to long-term client sustainability.

Setting Up Your First Ad

If you still haven't downloaded "Facebook Adverts Manager" to your phone, take a moment to do so now. Once you have downloaded the App, open it up and look for a plus sign (+) that says "Create Ad" or "Create a Campaign." This is where you will be faced with a handful of choices which I will outline below. No matter which one of these choices you make, you're only 3 to 4 steps away from having your Ad seen in your local Facebook feed.

Choice #1 - Boost a Post

This is an option Facebook gives you to show a post you've previously made on Instagram or Facebook, and have it be seen by everyone you advertise to (hopefully, local clients who can get to your salon.) I suggest only boosting your posts that have already received great feedback.

The downside of this option is that the "call now" and "book now" feature is not available for posts that have been posted before creating the Ad. That's why you hear about people who "boost" their posts but are missing out on the call to action buttons. Viewer who like the artists' work cannot immediately book an appointment, so they keep on scrolling.

For this reason, Choice #1 isn't necessarily ideal. I recommend you use the feature called "drive traffic to your website."

Choice #2 - Drive Traffic Feature

This is the not-so-secret option of creating a proper Facebook Ad campaign for your services. I strongly encourage you to use this feature and couple a video of a before and after transformation with the ad. In this post there will be a button that you can to link to your phone or your booking site.

If rule #1 of marketing is to create awareness, rule #2 is to grab clients' attention and have them come your way. When you target a female Facebook audience of 18 to 40 years of age and fund it with only $10 per day, you're looking at creating awareness for your services for hundreds or thousands of women per day, depending on where you live.

In the previous chapter, I was teaching you the strategy to use whatever free time you have, even if only 30 minutes per day to invest in your business with no budget. In this chapter, you are going to be putting your money where your mouth is, much like I did, to guarantee that your favourite Instagram or Facebook posts will specifically be seen by an audience that can walk or drive to you in a reasonable amount of time.

Wherever you may live, remember that half of those people are usually women, and most of them are already spending, on average, hours a day on their social media accounts. Paying to play on Facebook means that while you're at work working or at home sleeping, your ad scours for local clients and shows up in their feed every second of every day for as long as you run that ad.

Truly, I'm running out of words to describe how fantastic Facebook Ads can be for your business.

Creating Your Ad

Once you have selected either of the choices above (and I hope you decided choice #2), you will have an option of picking what you want to show to future local clients. Remember to pay attention to what clients are looking for in your area as well as what content you have that already performs well. For instance, it's the summer of 2017 as I'm writing this, and unicorn hair is slowly on its way out; trends are changing towards natural hair. Therefore, there are a lot of color corrections to be had. If that's your specialty, make sure you specify in your ad that you are a color correction specialist.

Once you've selected what you want to advertise to your future local clients, you will be brought to a screen inside the Facebook Adverts Manager where you can add a short description and set up your booking site to link out from Facebook. Here is where you will also be able to choose where your ad is placed, either Instagram or Facebook or BOTH. At the bottom, you will see a preview of what your ad looks like to your local neighbors, a.k.a. your future clients.

Choosing Your Audience

This is the 3rd and most important step to creating an Ad campaign, where you choose your audience of women or men, their age range, and what interests you want Facebook to recognize them by. Be sure to double check that the location is set up to your local area, I suggest no more than

30 miles away from your salon; this will ensure that Facebook only shows Ads to people who can actually reach your salon.

If you are wondering what you should choose for interests I recommend "online shopping" because there is a higher chance that women who shop online will press the button to book an appointment with you, so your advertising dollar will go further. For efficiency's sake, I suggest you create a new audience group and name it something like "19 - 40 female Your Local Area." Facebook Ads even work well in smaller towns, down to about 10,000 people in the area - meaning it works almost everywhere in the U.S and Canada.

What's incredible about Facebook Ads is the ability of a small business, like a self-employed hairstylist, to get the attention of so many local potential clients all at once. It's so much easier nowadays to grow your business. Remember that you're not in the business of selling physical goods; you're in the business of selling your time for services, which means your time is limited. I'll talk later about pricing that time appropriately (and maybe giving yourself a raise), but before that, I want to make sure you are strengthening your clientele using Facebook Ads.

CHAPTER 12

How to Caption Your Social Media Posts

At this point you know that every post you make or share on social media, whether it's a photo or video, requires a caption. Technically, you don't have to caption if you don't want, but the whole point of the sharing mechanisms of Facebook and Instagram is to briefly explain what your takeaway is from the content you are sharing with others. In this chapter, I will focus on the do's and don'ts of a social media caption. Your social media strategy will be so much easier if your content relates to people in a way that you also relate to. Otherwise it can feel uneasy and weird.

Before I dive into what works and doesn't work for me, I want to give you a quick breakdown of a caption's formula, which revolves around an old school marketing/advertising technique known as AIDA. This technique has been used for nearly 100 years by professional marketers and branding experts, and it is easy for you to use as well, even without marketing experience.

The AIDA Caption Formula

For as long as there has been advertising, there have been certain structures for how information has been presented. AIDA is the easiest one to explain and replicate as a beginner.

AIDA = Attention, Interest, Desire, Action

These are essential elements in any advertising effort, free or paid, short or long.

ATTENTION - First, you must attract the attention of your audience, in this case through social media posts.

INTEREST - Second, the post must arise the interest of that audience.

DESIRE - Third, that interest will create a desire to follow up with your services. This is where most hairstylists who post online stop.

ACTION - Just because you've made the post, and potential clients have found that post interesting, doesn't mean they will take action on that interest. You actually have to state in your captions something along the lines of "I'm available to discuss a potential color correction on your hair, so click the link in profile or call me at XXX-XXX-XXXX." This is called a "call to action."

Using this formula on your social media captions will increase engagement with your followers. Believe it or not, most people will not take action or contact you even if you have sparked their desire to have their hair done by you. They need to know what to do next after seeing your post. A well written caption can make your audience care about you, but without actionable steps on what to do next, their brain will go "ok, cool" and they will keep on swiping their screen. You must tell your audience what to do next in order to keep their attention and turn them into clients!

DO'S and DONT'S of an Instagram Caption

DO keep it simple. I find that the easier and lighter you keep the caption, the better the response will be to the post. Remember that the video or photo is the main attraction. Naturally, people will want to know the "who, what, when, and why" of the hair transformation. So, take your audience on a short journey by storytelling how the client felt before and after. Don't forget to tag the client as well.

DON'T write walls of text. Walls of text are called walls for a reason. They feel like one big blurb patched together and are hard to read. I prefer no more than two sentences per paragraph. My favorite strategy for keeping captions concise is to say as much as I need to get my point across, but not enough for it to feel overwhelming. If you're a wall-text kind of person, simply ensure that your social media posts from here on out have some spaces in between them. That'll be a good start.

DO use emojis. Emojis can definitely be overused, but they can also be underused. For the purpose of using them to ensure I don't create a wall of text, I insert one emoji in the line between paragraphs. This helps keep the caption clean, separates your text, and, when placed properly, will look good on all devices.

My favorite emoji is the pointing down finger because it sends a subconscious and colorful signal to your audience to keep reading your caption. Note that if your call to action is typically on the last line of your caption, your audience will have to hit "see more" to see it. In which case, suggesting that they keep reading is a good idea.

DO insert a call to action in every caption. Whether your intent is to reach out to current or new clients, you should always include a call to action. This can be something as soft as "tag a friend," or as hard as an appointment sell; however, I recommend that you only include a hard sell every 8-10 posts, which average out to about once a week. Only a small percentage of your posts should broadcast your intent to fill up your appointment book.

DON'T hard sell too frequently. The majority of your posts should contain calls to action that build your brand long-term instead of your client book directly. Think brand building. Not every post has to have a sales pitch in it. Most posts can simply include the client's instagram profile and a shoutout. Smart clients will check-in with that person privately and ask them about your services (social proof) and perhaps will message you for an appointment after.

Clients understand that you need to promote your services, but they can also be annoyed if you make too many blatant appointment posts, especially ones that straight out offer discounts.

DO post hashtags in the comments. If you plan on using more than 3-5 hashtags, you will create a cleaner post if you list them in your the comment section. Take a look at any popular Instagram account, and you will notice that if they use hashtags, they are usually listed in the comments section.

DON'T forget that your bread and butter will come from actually engaging with other people who use hashtags locally. Instagram has made it a lot easier to keep up with local posts, and you should take full advantage of that. You are, after all, a local business.

DO showcase the work you want to do. I built the Hairstylist Tribe Instagram platform on the idea of putting other hairstylists in the spotlight. As you grow your following, you may want to consider showcasing certain styles you feel comfortable doing, even if they belong to other stylists. By this I do not mean local shout outs (you don't want to drive business to your competitors). You should feature the work of hairstylists who are far enough that your clients won't be able to get to them.

This shows your followers what you are interested in and capable of doing. It basically says to your audience, "I know how to pull this off, come see me if you want your hair done like this!" When we share a post on social media, we're basically telling our audience that we approve and relate to whatever we are sharing. In a hair service situation, it says we feel comfortable we can achieve the same results.

Your local clientele are probably looking to keep up with the current trends and will consider you much more of an expert if you can confidently showcase a fellow hairstylist work on your platform, which in turn, helps you release more content, which takes the pressure off you creating your own content during slow times.

DO tag. Especially if the work does not belong to you, tag posts twice with the original artist's handle - once in the caption and once by actually tagging the photo. Also, be sure to tag clients when you post photos of their hair. This will make them feel special, keep them engaged in your work, and increase the potential that they will share your work with their friends.

DO'S and DON'TS of a Facebook Caption

Unlike Instagram, Facebook users are used to consuming longer form posts. This gives you the option to explore more storytelling techniques. It is true that higher engagement posts on Instagram tend to have long posts, but Facebook engagement rate is much higher.

As you may already know, the feeling of Facebook is different than Instagram. Facebook is a place where people do truly hang out and read stories. I see a lot of hairstylist friends on Facebook storytelling the transformation stories of their clients, and I hope more of you decide to take this route.

DO express express what your takeaway is. When people share a quote or a post on Facebook, they will often use more Instagram-appropriate captions like, "true" or "100." This doesn't engage your audience as well as a story explaining why you brought that quote or image to their attention. There needs to be a sort of emotional release on the part of the audience in order for people to relate to you.

I post hair features on Instagram that get hundreds of likes, but when I do post a business-related piece of content, I might only get 20 likes. The emotional connection with the work I share is much higher than with the less-sexy business advice. Even though the engagement is lower, I post business advice on purpose because I am trying to serve and educate those 20 people.

DON'T mass tag any more. One of the most annoying things on Facebook is being tagged alongside 20 other people in a products promotion. Do yourself a favour and don't start tagging every client or potential client you have on Facebook, it's the quickest way to lose followers.

DO mix up long and short captions. I find that videos don't need long captions because the content is built into the clip, however photos require you to tell the story in words. Long videos? Short captions. Short video or single photo post? Longer captions.

DO use links. It is much more professional to share links to articles on your Facebook page, as opposed to just sharing quotes. Bonus, Facebook offers increased organic reach for longer captions on its platform and less organic reach for pictures with quotes. When I see an article I like and want to share with all of you, I go to the original article, copy the link, and paste it straight into my post. This gives me a chance to express my takeaway and it increases the reach.

Links also make your actual post larger in the feed of your audience. When you're trying to keep your audience's attention in a fast scrolling digital world, you want to be able to take up as much as the screen as possible.

DO make your posts public. I learned this first hand when someone pointed out that they couldn't share my posts because they were set to only be seen by friends. The whole point of social media is to share, and if I make it hard for something I create to be shared, it defeats the whole purpose of me putting out content in the first place. Make it easy for people to share your art and you will find social media success.

DO use paragraph breaks. Similar to my advice about walls of text on Instagram, if you are going to tell a nice long story in writing on Facebook, a well known copywriting trick is to write a couple sentences per paragraph, then insert a blank space between each paragraph.

Walls of text on Facebook can give everybody the impression you are having a meltdown, similar to using caps lock to have an online discussion. Gaps between paragraphs give the reader a chance to catch their breath. Use them.

In closing...

Writing social media captions is one of the hottest topics everyone asks me about. Proper copywriting is a whole other conversation, but what you just learned from this chapter is a great foundation for effective captioning. Feel free to add your flavor, but just know that the easier and airier a caption is, the longer you will keep your audience's attention. You don't have to be a copywriter for this. Just follow my do's and dont's, and you will do well.

So remember - grab your audience's attention with an awesome photo or video, bring out their desire with your captions, and call them to action while saying as little as you can (but as much as you need) to get your point across.

CHAPTER 13

What Do the Instagram and Facebook "Metrics" Mean?

You may see notifications on Facebook encouraging you to boost your Ads. Whether you choose to pay for Instagram and Facebook advertising or not, you will see certain numbers and results being recorded for you.

In internet marketing lingo, the numbers for different data mechanisms on social media and their output are referred to as "metrics." Usually, people will focus on likes or impressions or reach, but those usually only describe one result out of the many metrics available. In other words, "likes" is only one way to measure what's working and what isn't.

Instagram Metrics Basics

Likes

This was originally Instagram's only engagement metric. With the current Instagram technology, we are not only able to see who liked, but also how many people were exposed to the post, i.e. reach. A good engagement ratio between likes and reach should be somewhere at 5%, meaning if 5% of your reach was likes, then you made a post that people can relate to and should continue to make similar posts.

It's important to focus on likes, but you should also now focus on the reach as well. Here's why…

Reach

According to Instagram, reach is the "number of unique accounts who saw your post." In order to consider a post successful, the reach should be 5% or higher. There are a few ways to increase your reach, and my favorite one is to spend a few dollars per day so that more of my Tribe sees my post.

I'm comfortable with the paid reach solution, and, personally, I feel that waiting around for organic reach is a waste of my time. Reach is the numbers of eyes that saw a post - the more people who see my posts, the better my brand building efforts become.

Engagement

Instagram refers to engagement as "the number of times your post was liked, saved, and commented on." Engagement is the new like. Social media is no longer as linear as people think - engagement is the most important metric for any piece of content. Sometimes I get a low number of likes, but I get more shares and more messages in my inbox because of the content I share. So to me, one message in response to my comment is more worthwhile than a whole bunch of likes. A message indicates that the content I posted made an impact.

Depending on the content you share across your platforms, you will also see these types of trends pop up. So as far as reading and understanding your data better, it makes sense to focus your energy on increasing the engagement numbers, not just likes.

Paid Instagram Metrics

While I highly recommend that you run your Instagram posts through your Facebook Ad account, but no matter where you start the ads, once the promotion runs it will start showing you results in a few hours. If you follow the basic advice in this book, you will most likely see overall results on your account within days.

One super important thing to remember is that your advertising campaigns from both Facebook and Instagram will be visible in the Facebook ads app. Make sure you download this App!

Facebook Ads App Domination

There are many more metrics available to you in the Facebook Adverts Manager app once you run an ad campaign. These metrics alone are worth the cost of a $5 ad because they are more in depth than the numbers you see inside the Instagram App. These can be found in the "Results" section.

Facebook refers to results as "the number of outcomes you achieved with your Ad based on the objectives you selected." Inside these metrics dashboards, you will see specific numbers and results which are not given to you if your post wasn't promoted. Below I cover a few important results and what they mean to you:

Frequency

Frequency is the "the average number of times each person saw your Ad." One of my recent ads had one of the highest frequencies ever, where a small reach of 20,000 yielded a frequency of 1.86 which meant each one of those 20,000 people saw the ad 1.85 times.

The idea behind frequency is to keep it under 2.0. The higher your frequency is, the more your posts have been seen by the same people multiple times. If your objective is to get fresh eyes on your posts, then you know that the high-frequency post should be used in a strategy where you want your *existing* audience to see your content because they already know you.

Relevant Score

This isn't something that is widely discussed in social media circles - but here is what relevant score really is - a number on a scale of 1 to 10, where ten means that your paid ad is showing to the right people, and 1 means it's showing to the wrong people.

Any number between 6 and 10 means that your Ad is showing to the audience you asked Facebook to show it to, and you are a few small tweaks away from getting it up to 10. As long as your Ad relevance score stays above 6, I recommend you let it run and create new Ads for that same audience so you have a basis of comparison in the future.

This is a important part of the results section of your Facebook and Instagram advertising. So remember that the higher your relevant score is, the higher your engagement will most likely be.

Post Reactions

Reactions quantifies the total engagement within an Ad campaign. It is the total number of shares, comments, and likes the Ad receives. It is in your best interest to share content that will get the highest number of reactions, whether you're running free or paid marketing.

Link Clicks

Most advertising campaigns on Facebook and Instagram will require you to define an outside link, like your booking site. Basic internet marketing teaches you to compare the amount of money you're spending on Ads to the metric that shows how many people clicked on the Ad.

An acceptable ratio of proper Ads spend is an average of $1 per one click. For Facebook and Instagram that is a WIN! You should celebrate when your link clicks cost way under $1 and rethink either your targeting or your budgeting if you start paying more than $2 per click.

It's important to mention that these numbers, statistics or data points (whatever you want to call them) exist on Instagram in order to give you, the account owner, an idea of how well your social media profile is doing. Without them, we would never know how many people see our posts, what percentage of them liked what we post, or how many people click and take action.

These numbers tell you how "healthy" your profile is and give you an indication of how well your audience can relate to your content, so it's important that you, the creative type, take the time to understand this math. The better you understand your social media numbers, the better you will know what and what not to post, which gives you a better chance of attracting the right clientele...in turn improving your bank account numbers!

Unfortunately, we cannot run away from math and numbers, so the best thing to do is face it head on and learn them in order to build a better business. If statistics were not important to a business, they wouldn't exist on the Instagram platform.

CHAPTER 14

The Customer Journey Now Starts on Social Media

One of the perks of having built a community like Hairstylist Tribe is every time I need to "renovate" my hair whether it's an A-line bob (I love bobs) or a color correction, I get to pick and choose from a community of thousands of hair professionals.

I start what is called the consumer journey long in advance of booking a consult. What I usually do is check what city I'm going to be in, and I find all the hairstylists I can within our Tribe that look like they could do what I want. I find hairstylists who post often on Instagram and who specialize in what I'm looking for. I search for hairstylists who communicate to me through photos and videos what they care about the most when it comes to hair.

What I noticed about my experience having my hair done recently by a hairstylist whom I haven't met was I was able to trust her *months* in advance of meeting her. Which leads me to the theme of this chapter: trust. You might already know this but, most clients have trust issues, even if they don't seem like they do. Before the internet, there was no real way to build up trust with a beauty professional. You could get referrals or see photos in flyers, but all the action was in the salon. That was the original consumer journey - all offline and that's all there was.

Things Have Changed (Thankfully)

The consumer experience (also known as the user journey) starts online first before it goes offline to the salon. Potential customers no longer begin their experience the moment they walk into your place of business; they begin their customer journey before you are even aware of their existence, as they're looking at your social media account. They start creeping your social media platforms and sizing you up long before they enter your experience.

I've identified Four Steps in the online part of the consumer journey from "I had an idea to get my hair done" to "I just got my hair done."

1. The Trigger - Something makes the client feel that they want to get their hair done.

2. Exploration & Research - Usually right after the Trigger moment, they start searching and sorting through all the hairstylist social media profiles.

3. Decision Making - The next measurable moment is when they decide on which hair professional will do their hair - usually it is something specific on the stylist's online portfolio that made that client tick.

4. Action Taking (Reservation- or Appointment-making) - The final measurable moment in the consumer journey is the first moment of contact, when the client decided to message you.

Let's take my personal journey to get my hair done recently as the example.

It was late November, and I knew I wanted to color my hair in March. For me to feel confident that my hair would still be healthy after that hair service, I had to feel comfortable with the work of whoever was going to do my hair. In this case, I needed a color specialist who did kick ass purples and cared about hair health in the Vancouver area (Canada).

After navigating Hairstylist Tribe and going through my search (aka creeping) process, by early December, I zeroed in on a stylist and decided to direct message her. That same day, I decided I trusted her enough to set up an appointment. Given her super professional Instagram profile and her involvement as a teacher in our industry, my anxiety levels lowered and my trust level increased instantly when I viewed her profile.

All this is part of the consumer journey - these things happen before the client even sits in your chair. Clients creep your work and establish their level of trust for you in their heads before you even hear know they exist.

Something Changed When the Internet "Happened"

Be mindful that the consumer journey starts the moment a client looks in the mirror in the privacy in their home and says to themselves, "I need to get my hair done, I'm going to look at Instagram for 3 hours until I find someone I trust."

We also have to understand as an industry that there is a type of rational conversation the client has with themselves as they are creeping social media hair accounts. Consumers start their relationship with you, the hair professional, the moment they lay eyes on your Instagram account. Even a walk-in who decided that same morning she was going to do something about her hair usually creeps multiple hair accounts before walking in without an appointment. Whether a client books with you three months or three days in advance or you get a cold walk-in, you damn well better know that they stalked you all over the internet.

Those local hashtags we all take for granted make so much it easier for potential local clients to trust most beauty professionals and we don't even realize it. No client hangs out in the Google search bar - they spend time on Instagram and Facebook. If you think reviews of your services are important, imagine how deep clients go to look at the details of your professional life - even your personal life.

You must be willing to put yourself in the mindset of a customer and understand how they behave online before they reach out to you. In other words, how would you act? Too many beauty professionals are concerned about how they're going to act around their customers while in the salon, but what they should focus on is creating a good first impression before they even meet their clients.

Again, there used to be only one type of customer experience - in-person, offline experiences where clients had no idea what stylists were capable of before the appointment. However, as I write this in 2017, there is a new layer that has been added to the customer journey which is an online component. It's been around for years and isn't going anywhere. Social media not only allows the client to start the consumer journey in the privacy of their phone, but it also gives you the ability to prepare and position your online portfolio such that the client knows what to expect before they even call for an appointment.

My consumer journey with the hairstylist I mentioned above started long before I sat in her chair. When I finally did, it was a pleasure because my interaction with her online portfolio allowed me to build trust. I hadn't met this person yet, but because of the way she positioned her profile I trusted her more then hairstylists I've known in person for years.

Pre-appointment trust matters a whole lot than we think - it certainly matters to me as the client. So put yourself in the mindset of a customer and ask yourself, "How would I behave between the time I decide I need my hair done and the time I book an appointment with an actual hairstylist?" I'm convinced you'll have an easier time handling clients in the future if you remember what they go through mentally before they reach out to you.

CHAPTER 15

How to Keep Productivity High and Stress Less

Okay, this is a chapter where you can take a breath. Go put the tea on, make yourself a coffee, get a snack, and try to spend some time digesting everything you've read in this book up until now. Then come back read this short chapter and get inspired to finish reading. If you're super ramped up at this point, now is a good time to go back to the beginning and start following along by actually implementing some of the advice. This is the chapter that separates the general advice in the previous 14 chapters from the rest of the book.

Start putting social media to work for you but getting into a routine, a system, this new habit we are all trying to get a grasp of called "living in a 24/7 digitally connected world," something that growing up only two decades ago sounded like technology out of a Scifi movie. For those of you that sometimes feel like throwing your phone against the wall because text messages and calls won't stop coming in, creating a little social media business diet might help you stay more organized.

My word of advice is to try to enjoy learning social media as you would learn how to play a sport or an instrument. It really doesn't have to feel like this awkward public forum that everyone makes it seem like. We have to be realistic and understand that clients now more than ever shop digitally, and there is nothing that we can do to make it go back to the way things used to be.

Frustrating but Worth It

Like any other skill, if you give social media skills the attention they need, you can actually let resistance fall away and let your creativity flourish. As you eagerly reawaken your drive to improve your social media game, I want you to remember one thing : have patience.

It's not a sprint, it's a marathon. Running even one simple Facebook Ad with the suggestions I've made throughout the book will put you and your social media profiles in front a handful of people. That's all you really need: 5, 10, 15 more clients. You're better off finding 20 new clients then 20,000 random followers. And that's why I want you to stress less - you need to remember that you're not looking for thousands of clients the way other businesses like an e-commerce shop are. If you have two slow days, you only need a hand-full of clients to fill up your schedule!

I didn't write this book to teach you how to be a wealthy hairstylist; I wrote this book to unlock your mind to vast new opportunities that give you endless avenues to becoming wealthy. I want to ease your mind and leave you with this last piece of advice, wherever you are at in your social media growth: stop worrying and focusing on what someone else is doing on their accounts. Take satisfaction is knowing that you are also learning how to use social media to your advantage!

Just focus on the process - habits take time to build.

CHAPTER 16

How to Use the Internet
to Generate Business in
a Rural Area

Although the majority of the human population congregates in and around large cities, small towns and underpopulated areas are still open for business, and hairstylists and cosmetologists still exist there. This is why I've decided to dedicate this particular chapter to the beauty professionals and the salon owners outside of the large metro areas. If you live in a city or town with under 50,000 people, this chapter will benefit you in more ways than one.

One of the advantages of working online and coaching hair professionals is I get to take my work everywhere I go. It's how I chose to design my life, and I'm forever grateful that I'm able to give back to so many in our industry. This puts me in a position to fully understand the different dynamics of small and large cities alike.

However, between large metro areas, there are thousands and thousands of small towns lodged alongside the interstates and freeways that crisscross this beautiful continent. Our industry has this unique ability to glamorize places like New York, Las Angeles, and all the other major cities where everything moves fast, but it doesn't mean that the 5,000-person-towns in the middle of the country should be ignored and remain uninformed.

Most of the stylists on our Hairstylist Tribe platform are actually living outside major urban areas. And while it may seem harder for them to find new clients, it's important stay in the game and ignore the people telling you there is nothing you can do about it. There is. There always is.

Don't Run Ads (Wait, What?)

I know, I know...

This book is about social media advertising but if you're in a rural area, I advise against advertising online - at least not right away. I suggest you take a different approach. Believe me, I'm not trying to confuse you or contradict myself. It's just the truth for small town salon businesses is you must deploy different strategies which include more face-to-face interaction and in-person meetings.

As much as I love mass-scale advertising and the social-media-based attention grabbing, what I would recommend to these small town salons, is to connect with other businesses in their town, face-to-face. You should use the internet to find information about these others businesses in order to better prepare a cross-promoting strategy, but the approach must be different. These other local businesses aren't going to be your clients. They are going to be your allies in helping you attract more clients - their clients.

What I suggest is you reverse engineer a clientele by reaching out to businesses that already active online. The more active they are on Google, Yelp, or Facebook, the more likely they are to be open to whatever ideas you come up with. Contrary to popular belief, the majority of businesses out there still don't believe in this "internet thing" as much as some of us do, but they are slowly coming around to embracing it. You have to be an internet ally in their circle of influence.

I'm well aware of the fact that the smaller a town is, the more people know one another. But since this is a book about online marketing, I want you to do the legwork online before you approach other businesses in person. I want you to treat Google like the Yellow Pages of your local town and find as much information on the business and the person behind it on Instagram, Facebook, Yelp and even from your local Chamber of Commerce if you can.

In rural areas, there are businesses that understand the concept of cross promoting which, strangely enough, no longer works as well in large cities. In large cities, things move way too fast for cross promoting, but in small towns it is still a part of daily business life. But before you start approaching other local businesses, you must first do your homework on them. If there are 50 businesses in your town, 15 of them might be a good fit for your salon, and it's up to you to put in some time each day to figure out who these business may be.

The best thing to do is grab a list of all the registered businesses in your town, county, or zip code from the county office or city hall and go through them. You can even download them from their website since all of this information is public record.

Once You Have the Information...

Once you know which businesses you would like to work with, contact the managers or business owners and float the idea of cross promotion.

Now I'm not going to get into details of cross promoting because there are thousands of ways you can do this, but the number-one thing you have to find in any business you want to cross promote with is a willing business owner.

As you do your research, consider creating a simple spreadsheet (Google Drive is a free platform), or even creating a list of businesses you would be interested in cross promoting in your phone. This will help you stay organized, and you'll easily be able to access your information and remember details about all your business allies.

Show Other Business Owners What You Can Do for Them

When you're the first one to reach out to another business, you might think that you're doing both of you a favor, but the other business owner may not understand the benefits at first. Be prepared to explain to them what is it that you are trying to achieve and what you are willing to offer. People don't care about what you can do for yourself, they care what you can do for them.

Given the fact that smaller towns have less reach on social media advertising platforms, you can't go at it alone. So the small-town community mentality will work more in your favour the less populated your zip code is. It's not as important to figure out the perfect strategy as it is for you to do your research, reach out, and open a conversation with those other businesses. You have to find another business that meshes well with your business and remember that a business is an expression of another human being's desires and actions. Businesses are run by people not robots, so start nurturing those relationships now.

Connect first and foremost with the businesses owners that are willing to accept that the Internet is not a fad. You can tell right away by whether or not they have an online presence.

While they don't have to be tech savvy, they should be open to it. Whether it's the town gym or the coffee shop next door, the number-one thing that will tell you if the business cross promoting efforts will be successful long term is if the other business owner is open minded.

Last winter we had the pleasure of spending a few months in the town of Tofino on Vancouver Island on the West coast of Canada. While in town we met a business owner who would go from business to business convincing the owners to join her small Facebook Page and Facebook Group. That is an open-minded business owner.

Being open to working with other businesses gave her the ability to speak to individual business owners about growing their online presence, together as a business community. That allowed her to create her own circle of influence, all through cross promotion.

Become the Local Social Media Expert

The biggest piece of advice I have for you is to consider becoming the social media expert in your town, even if your town is small.

At some point, businesses that don't close will realize that social media is a fantastic way of attracting more clients, and if you stay on top of it and organize small informal business owner gatherings, you will eventually become the go-to marketing guru in your town.

Create Sneezers (aka Influencers)

In his book, The Idea Virus, Seth Godin describes "sneezers" as people who tell everyone about your services wherever they go. They tell everyone about their life experiences, all the places they visit, the people they see, and all the things they buy. If you recognize and treat these individuals well, you can bet they will tell everyone in town about you and your salon business.

In the Influencer chapter later in this book, I mention that sneezers are to be taken seriously in large cities because of their social media popularity. If you're in a small town, the popular sneezers may be the real estate agent who knows everybody or the grocery store manager. Start a relationship with them. Instead of handing out business cards and spending time and money advertising on your local radio or TV station, spend a few hours with these word-of-mouth sneezers. Personal relationships are what builds businesses the best, not flyers.

These people know everybody. If you're fortunate enough to have a few clients who behave this way, and you're in their good graces, they're more likely to tell everyone about you, so be aware of this small distinction the next time you interact with your current clients. Do you have a client who seems to speak about everything and everybody? They are most likely a sneezer and if given the chance, they will influence other locals' buying decisions. Treat them extra-well, and in time they will tell everyone they meet and know about you.

Small Town Living Is an Advantage

I can see how, living in a small town, it may often feel like the grass is greener on the other side. It may seem like you aren't able to build a proper clientele the way you would in a large city. Yes, the opportunities are more abundant in a huge city, and it feels like everyone and anybody can become your client, but the turnover is also greater. In a small town you have the advantage of creating more one-on-one interactions with people, and you may do so much faster. These relationships may last longer than in a city where people are constantly having other salons and services dangled in their face, often on social media.

At the end of the day, it's a matter of perspective so I don't want you to get caught up in a frenzy of negative self-talk, trying to tell yourself that it's much harder for you because you live in a small town. I want you to try and give it your all.

Business-building and clientele-building are very controllable, and I hope you take this chapter as an outline of what to do in order to get the wheels rolling to secure your spot as the go-to business builder and networking expert in your town. Add your own flavour to it, spice it up, and make it unique to you. Plenty of hairstylists have been successful growing their clientele out of a few clients living in a small town.

CHAPTER 17

Social Media Strategies for Salon Owners

The biggest problem I see salon owners having with social media is their inability to convince or the unwillingness on the part of the hairstylist to cooperate by contributing to the growth of the salon's social media pages.

I know first hand just how frustrating it can be to get anybody else other than yourself to care as much as you do about the marketing and branding well-being of a salon. One thing I learned when I filled in for the salon manager is the harsh truth that nobody cares about the salon as much as the owner does. Not even the employees who benefit from the salon being open.

Your Employees Don't Care As Much As You Do

At some point in our lives, we all realize that no one cares as much about us as they do about themselves. They may tell you they do, but they don't.

A simple empathy exercise will help you internalize this simple truth, and you will be a better leader for it. When I'm asked, "How do I convince the hairstylists who work under me to post on the salon social media pages?"

The answer is simple: You don't.

But there is a cool mental hack that will free you of that anxiety and frustration. Instead of convincing, compromising, and even threatening your employees to care about you salon social media pages as much as you do, do this instead:

Encourage them to share their work to their own social media platforms as much as possible. This frees them from feeling as if they are letting you down or overwhelmed by posting to the salon page. Then have whoever runs your social media accounts follow your own employees' accounts, screenshot their photos, and repost them on your salon social media pages with proper credits.

With this simple mindset shift, you can now focus on how to take the photos that you shared on your Facebook and Instagram and run Facebook and or Instagram Ads to grow your local clientele. It is your duty as the salon owner, as the business person trying to keep the business growing to do everything in your power to market and advertise non-stop. Employees and booth renters only care about their own social media pages, and you have to be okay with that. What you should not be okay with is leaving the marketing and branding up to your employees.

This chapter isn't about cutting your employees slack, it's about giving yourself a break from the unnecessary and mundane conversations about social media with your employees. I'd much rather you focus that energy on the creative alternative I offered you because you know what, it's much easier for the hairstylist to be encouraged to share their work on their very own accounts than to create the expectation for them of having to carry the burden of creating content for your business.

As much as I want your life to be easier, you also have to understand that your employees don't need the added workload of posting on your salon social pages AND their own pages - it's your salon after all. I'm a huge fan of teamwork, and everyone has their own way of doing things on their own social profiles, but sometimes discussions of "teamwork" can walk a fine line between good intent and peer pressure. This can lead to your employees feeling stressed and burnt out.

I highly recommend that you take a couple of hours out of your day to share your staff's work or hire a social media marketing expert that can assist you on a daily basis; just don't put the burden on your employees.

Remember...

All investments you make for the betterment of the salon are tax deductible. It's easier to run advertising campaigns and/or hire professionals to help you share content so you can focus on serving your growing clientele.

As the adage goes, "you have to spend money to make money." Facebook and Instagram advertising are a powerhouse of platforms where your marketing dollar will go far, especially when you craft and advertise the right offers and campaigns.

How to Find Ideal Employees Through Social Media

Owners often ask me how to find the best possible employees/booth renters for their salons. To that question, I have a two-part answer.

First, as a business owner you must realize that no employee will ever care about your own business as much as you do - it's just not going to happen. Not in the beauty industry, not in the fitness industry, not anywhere. I know it sounds negative, but it's easy to theoretically understand this concept without really letting it sink in. The fastest way to get over this hang-up is to you to put yourself in your employee's shoes and ask yourself, "do I care about my workplace as much as my employer does?"

Actually, you want to care more about your business than your employees do. If employees cared as much as you did, then it means that you have a broken business because you obviously don't care enough. If your employees are more driven and invested, you may want to ask yourself why you are in business in the first place. And you better believe that employees who openly care about the business equally or more than their boss already ask themselves the same question.

I came to this realization during my last few years working in a salon full-time when I was given the responsibility of indirectly managing the salon. I didn't know much about management, but once I got up to speed I realized that my boss expected me to care more about his business then he did. It was strange and wrong.

Expecting your employees to care about your business as much as you do puts you in a vulnerable position to eventually be taken advantage of, lose employees, or worse the business will shut down, as it happened at my salon. The unspoken rule of business is that leaders are always expected to take on the pressure, worries, and cares of the business in order for everyone to operate fruitfully. Your employees are your employees for a reason. They look up to you to be the most responsible one out of them all. Don't place that burden on them.

On the Other Hand

Being an a-hole boss is just as bad as being a pushover. You can't have it both ways, but you can find the middle ground. Regardless of skill and talent level, you will always care more than your employees and you need to make sure that they know that. But that's no reason to be a jerk. If your employees had to care about your business as much as you think they should plus they have to deal with an aggressive, dismissive employer, they'd be better off running their own business.

Know that You Work for Them

Here's a concept that might rub you the wrong way, but I assure you it will lower your stress levels once you fully accept it - you are not the boss of your employees, they are the boss of you. You are the one that everything falls on 24/7. If your employee is an a-hole, it is your fault that you've allowed them to be without repercussions. So talk it out with them or get rid of them.

When you remove the importance that society has placed on hierarchy and think about it logically, you realize that you need your employees, not the other way around. You are the one who has the business, the responsibilities, and the bills to keep your business running. Your employees can up and leave at any moment, and they will if you are a weak leader, regardless of what your arrangements with them may be.

You have to understand that nobody benefits from the rewards of your business like you do which means your employees simply won't care as much. They will usually only do enough to get through each day. They have yet to take the sort risks that come with running a legal business like you did. It's good or bad, it's just the truth. I have been an employee and even though I cared about my workplace, I can tell you I never cared about the salon as much as I care about Hairstylist Tribe, my baby that I imagined, started, and invested in.

Most stylists haven't taken the risks of business ownership, because they prefer less responsibility and stress. They prefer working under someone who can shelter them from the responsibilities of day-to-day business management and just want to have a place they can go everyday without the added worries of being a business owner.

People Change, So Change Your Game

Obviously, I am generalizing the dynamics of employer/employee relationships. But, many salon owners have messaged me about this dilemma over the last few years and in our discussions I have discovered what most of them have yet to understand this about their staff.

What they did not understand is that in order to find quality staff, owners must subjugate their egos, step off their pedestals, and realize that employees will not come find you. You need to work hard to find them. There are a ton of salons out there, so you need to do everything in your power to ensure yours stands out.

I see so many salon owners out there complaining about not being able to find the right staff for their salon, and in my head I often ask myself when I see this, "I wonder how hard they tried?"

Thank Goodness for Social Media

The past is the past, and the future is unknown, but in our present, we have these things called social media platforms where you can find entire groups with tens of thousands of beauty professionals, many of whom are also always searching for a better workplace - use these platforms! Join 30 Facebook hair groups if you have to and start scouting for new employees the same way colleges scout for athletes every single year. However, unlike those college scouts, you don't even have to travel. You have a smartphone that travels with you everywhere instead.

Fortunately for you, there are hundreds of thousands of hair professionals that check their Facebook and Instagram an average of 30 times a day. So put in the research and work, and remember it's only a matter of time.

Control Your Business, Don't Let It Control You

Much like an independent hairstylist uses social media to find clients, you must use social media to find your ideal staff. In the same way that independent hairstylists showcase their work to future clientele, you have to showcase your salon, culture, and rules to the rest of the community.

It sounds harsh, but sitting around and complaining that you live in a place where you can't find the right staff is disempowering to you personally. Regardless of whether it's true or not, you have only two choices: you can either find the right staff to come to you, or you can move your business to a place with a larger pool of hair professionals.

As an example, Orange County California has close to 1,000 licensed hairstylists.

If you are passionate for the industry, but the market for hairstylists or cosmetologists is nonexistent where you live, you either find a way to convince people to come to you, or you take your business where the action is. Like California.

In our fast-paced world where employee turnover rate is under 18 months, the only way you'll stay afloat and in business is if you adapt. Once you're willing to do what it takes to be a successful business owner, then you're in a position to consider all of the options available, not just the ones that mean you get to stay where you're at.

Money, Money, Money

You can't remain emotionally addicted to your salon owner status. It takes humility to do what's necessary to keep your business running - which is anything and everything! There are hundreds of ways to run your business, but the number one thing that never changes in our global economy is supply and demand. When there is a shortage of hairstylists, you either move to where most of them are, or you play the cards you've been dealt.

But what I want from you more than anything, is to lower your stress and anxiety levels, which are usually the products of being overly romantic about how you run your business. Just face the situation for what it is. If your salon is in a rural area, the reason you have a shortage of staff is that most of them probably moved to the closest city because that's where the job opportunities are.

You really have to assess your salon situation and figure out why is it that you can't find staff. I will tell you right now, in 2017 as I'm writing this book, it's easier than ever to at least have conversations with hundreds if not thousands of potential staff members. I've done it, so can you - no matter where you are.

On the flip side, if your salon is in a larger city, you have to devise a plan for attracting the right staff members not only locally, but also nationally. Often times, potential employees will have an easier time moving across the country if your salon is in a major city. Take advantage of your big city salon location and keep on searching for the right staff members.

People Go Where Money Flows

It is only from a place of absolute truth, when you are fully and openly honest with yourself, that you'll make the best decision possible.

If Chris McMillan Salon in Beverly Hills was Chris McMillan Salon in Roseburg Oregon, he wouldn't be the Chris McMillan doing Jennifer Aniston's hair. (I have nothing against Oregon by the way, I love Roseburg.) I'm not saying that everyone needs to open a salon in Beverly Hills (remember, supply and demand), but if you are truthful with yourself and honest about what you're willing to do and not do, you will have less stress running your business.

Having said that, whatever town, city, or village your salon may be in, everything is finite. Which means that there is only so much available in terms of humans you can employ and clients you can attract. That's called human capital. I am not suggesting that you uproot your family, but what I am suggesting is that you have to consider what your local community can support when you are setting goals and expectations for your business.

Consider Doing Everything You Can

There are many owners who are happy closing their business and working for someone else because they can at least say that they've tried. I get it! Salon ownership is a great goals, but it's certainly not for everyone. However, if you're considering closing shop, before you do so be sure that you have tried everything to make it work.

Consider posting weekly job listing on twenty or so different hair groups for a year. Consider running Facebook Ads and placing them in front of the 1.3 million hair job titles in the U.S. You never know how many thousands of stylists and cosmetologists may be willing to move across the country to work in your business. It sounds cliche, but you don't know until you try. The hours you spend every day worrying about lack of staff can be spent productively in networking to find employees, exactly like you would network to find clients.

The higher the risks one takes, the larger the rewards become. That's why people open businesses, for the potential reward. As a business owner, however, this means that everything falls on you before it falls apart. That's why it's so hard when you own a salon and still work behind the chair.

The whole point of running a business is to fully dedicate your time, energy and resources to making the business work. This means you can not be a full-time stylist and a full-time salon owner. I have personally seen salon owners try to keep their role as hairstylist within their salon, and I have watched their salon fall apart as they were taking better care of their clients than their business and staff members.

This is a concept that the infamous Tabatha Coffey has tried to instill in our professional minds. In her TV show a few years ago, Tabatha's Salon Takeover, she would ask the salon owners who were still working behind the chair why they didn't have a separate salon manager. Most owners replied, not that they were trying to save money, but that they thought they could do both. They thought they could take on more than they could handle. Obviously, they couldn't or else they wouldn't have needed Tabitha's help!

My Soft Spot

I have a soft spot for the entrepreneurially-inclined hairstylist. I feel that if someone who cares about their financial well-being enough to start a business should have the best possible advice and strategies at their disposal.

Just how owners you work for their employees, I work for you, the salon owner, in order to make sure that you have the right strategies available and the proper perspective so that you can continue to run and grow your business. If I didn't care I wouldn't have written this book. Please consider my thoughts and advice on this matter; don't take them lightly. Your business depends on it.

CHAPTER 18

Social Media Advice for Freelancers and All Other Beauty Professionals

I would like to dedicate this short chapter to all the freelancers in the beauty industry who may or may not also do hair full time. I wanted to assure you that I know you exist. And there are many of you. While this book was intended to speak to mostly hairstylists, I haven't forgotten about makeup artists, nail techs, and other professionals in our industry.

You may be in a slightly different part of the beauty industry, or you may be bouncing between being a hairstylist and, say, makeup artist. Whatever the case, I see you, I hear you, and I know you're just as important as everyone else in the industry.

All of the concepts and actionable advice laid out in this book can serve you just as well as hairstylists or salon owners. At this point, like any other full-time hairstylist, you now have the tools and a well-organized step-by-step strategy for learning and applying the right techniques, at the right time, and in the right order. Whether you cut hair or do makeup, this book has given you the context and strategies with which you can create long-term business relationships with your clients. Our skills and talents may differ as professionals, but ultimately we are all in the service business.

To me, a freelancer is somebody that chooses not to work in a salon full-time. In our connected world, there are many job labels that people choose to apply to themselves, and while this book is aimed at hairstylists for the purpose of language simplicity, salon stylists aren't the only ones that can benefit from the content of these pages.

If you turned to this chapter because you consider yourself a freelancer, but haven't read the book from the beginning, feel better knowing that this book applies to you as much as it applies to hairstylists and salon owners. As long as clients shop for services online, they will always shop in the comfort and familiarity of their social media platforms. Just like a traditional salon stylist, you have to know remember and take advantage of this.

I believe you as a freelancer beauty industry professional hold an advantage over other artists, due to your ability to be mobile and flexible with your schedule. In a way, you are more entrepreneurial than any other professional in our industry because you are much more open to risk than someone with a stable location. For that, I applaud you!

CHAPTER 19

Social Media Formula for Educators

How to Find Other Professionals Who Want to Learn What You Know

Hairstylists looking to find other beauty professionals as their clients, can use the same advice from the rest of this book. In a way, educators are faced with the same social media dilemma we are facing here at Hairstylist Tribe.

If you're in the business of coaching and educating other hair professionals, you are in what's called a "business to business" (B2B) situation. You see, behind the chair, you are in a B2C (business to consumer). Hairstylist Tribe grew rapidly, in the B2B part of our industry. We don't sell to the end consumer; we sell to another business, which is usually a hairstylist or salon owner. When it comes to you advertising your services on social media, you must be aware of that distinction.

You're a Business-to-Business Provider

You are in a position where you must advertise your education services to others like you, and what better way to do so then doing what we do at Hairstylist Tribe?

At the time I'm writing this book, we are paying about 10 cents for every new hairstylist that sees our advertising and about 1 dollar for each one of them to join our email list. When you make the mindset shift in your marketing strategy and start advertising your professional education services to others in our industry, you'll build an audience of targeted hair professionals for pennies on the dollar, even compared to finding salon clients.

Salon clients are finicky - they jump ship often. If you want to become an industry educator, your work will be very specific, which means your audience will be very specific... which means that every single hairstylist beauty professional who likes your content and your brand is a much better lead then a potential client who can choose from hundreds of stylists in their area. You would not believe how many hair professionals message me privately on a weekly basis asking for recommendations on hair educators.

Hair educators are charging anywhere from $300 and up per head for you to attend their classes. Our industry is starving for educators, more so for educators who know how to market themselves to fellow hairstylists who are actually willing to pay and learn and grow.

When Others Say Advertising Makes You Look Desperate

You'll hear from other educators and people with large followings that advertising to grow your business somehow makes you look desperate. When you first hear this, I want you to think back to this book and imagine me giving that person the middle finger.

I cover this argument in a separate chapter, but you have to know that the people who say things like this about advertising are insecure and romantic about how they make their money - and eventually they will be left behind.

They tend to believe the larger their followings are, the more people are supposed to take them seriously, but when you take a look at their business model they're all doing sorts of "hope marketing." They are banking on a lot of people following them on social media in order to build their business, then lie to the rest of the world by claiming their business is doing well just because they have lots of followers online. That may work for some time, but what if social media changes? What then?

Stay away from people who say that advertising your services makes you look desperate. You have the opportunity to advertise for pennies on the dollar, find other hair professionals to educate, and hopefully, in time, the voices of the negative few will be drowned out. You can refer back to chapter 13 in order to better understand the numbers and the results you get from running your own Ads, but the number one thing that changes for an educator is you have to target others like you.

Remember, the goal isn't to target all women, the goal is to target all hair professionals who could benefit from your content and knowledge. I know this sounds too good to be true, but it's just how Facebook and Instagram operate. Facebook is a goldmine for reaching others like us.

Unless somebody is paying your bills, they have no right to tell you how to market yourself and what to do. Keep your chin up, stay focused, keep learning from people who are putting positivity into our industry, and don't forget to take everything everyone says with a grain of salt (including hairstylists with hundreds of thousands of followers).

I talk a lot about having an open mind and taking constructive criticism, but if you even hear a hairstylist with a large audience base spew negativity about the very platforms that help them become known, simply laugh at them and move on with your day. If they don't realize what they're saying, they really don't understand how they got to where they are in the first place, and their business is doomed whether they realize it or not. Is that someone you'd want to take advice from?

CHAPTER 20

Influencer Marketing: How to Ethically "Steal" Others' Followers and Turn Them Into Clients

Influencer Marketing

*I*n a nutshell, "influencer marketing" refers to a strategy where a brand, company, or even a small business pays an individual who has large followings on social media to share photos of or show up at a place of business in order for the influencer's followers to see it. Those followers then become aware of and potentially buy the endorsed product or service.

Over the last few years, you may have seen Instagram users that team up with other accounts in order to promote each other's work. This is loosely called "share for share," or "S for S." We originally built the Hairstylist Tribe Instagram out of this concept. What we did differently, however, was promote hairstylists who do great work in the hopes that they would share our page with their hairstylist friends. You, however, will have a much easier time connecting with influencers because of the strategy I'm about to lay out for you.

There's been a big influencer marketing push online by big brands. However, this strategy is a business growth solution for the average small business owner as well. The concept is simple - you find influencers, meaning people with 3,000+ followers, and you connect with them. You reach out to them and offer a service in exchange for appearing on their social media profiles. The reason you have it much easier than the big global brands is you only have to focus on your local area. This means you will only have to focus on finding local influencers.

These local influencers don't necessarily have to be celebrities. Influencers are usually mini-celebrities and are known to a few thousand locals, as opposed to millions of people globally. Find and connect with the people whose Instagram accounts are getting at least a few hundred likes a post. In this case you'll know that this person is active and has an engaged audience, regardless of whether they are globally famous or not. Influencers are famous to their audiences and that's quite enough.

Do a search of popular hashtags in your city and check out the popular posts. Those posts typically have high engagement because they are made by popular local accounts. Those are the accounts you have to focus on and create a relationship with. When you reach out to them, instead of immediately asking them to share your work on their page, offer them a good enough reason. Perhaps offer for them to come in and see you for services in exchange for posts about their experience. After all, influencers need their hair done just like everyone else.

These influencers most of the time will respond favorably because:

They understand what you are trying to do.

They do in fact secretly consider themselves an influencer.

They know hair services are expensive.

They are usually trying to offset some of their living expenses by leveraging their audience, but are not making enough income where they have the luxury of turning down your $ 100 - $1,000 service.

Be aware of the fact that these influencers are usually not multi-millionaires, but do have certain lifestyles they need to keep up with, which they do by promoting services and products on their social profiles. This is your greatest advantage in forging relationships with them.

Statistically, 89% of people who consider themselves influencers don't believe brands pay them enough. I'm not implying you should pay them cash, in fact, I believe you should barter your services for exposure on their platforms instead. Influencer marketing can cost you hundreds of dollars for a post, so I highly recommend that you take a couple days each month where you focus your attention on bartering with these influencers in order to grow your local follower base.

The followers that you attract will generally want to keep up with the influencer, in which case they will want to become your client as well. The clients that may come out of relationships you build with influencers will most likely remain long term clients. If you commit to a $300 service for the influencer, and you land 3 clients in the following weeks, you not only make back your money on the services you bartered, but those clients, by coming back, will multiply and pay back that bartering investment you made. This will continue to add up the more those clients come back in the future.

The Instagram influencers I want you to reach out to have thousands of eyes on their profiles. Next to Facebook Ads, influencer marketing is the next best word of mouth strategy. The more followers a local influencer has, the more people are going to see their hair. They are basically wearing your art 24/7. It's in your best interest to find these local celebrities and explain to them what you're willing to do (and not do, you certainly don't want to be taken advantage of) in exchange for them posting to their social media.

Focus on local personalities who may be personal trainers, restaurant owners, bloggers, or vloggers. These folks already understand about content distribution, positioning, photography, and lighting, which makes them easy to work with on social media. The more local they are, the more accessible they'll be.

If you work with an influencer that has 10,000 followers with 10% engagement on photos, that is 1,000 people who could potentially see your work on their idol's head. When those 1,000 people see this local celebrity's hair, they'll want to have their hair done by the same person. Remember that it's a numbers game, and if you can't afford the $100 - 300 per month for basic Instagram and Facebook Ads, then at least consider opening up a day in your calendar where you offer a service to an influencer. Spend time instead of money.

When You Are Cash-Strapped, Your Other Resource Is Time

Consider the kind of relationships you are going to be building with these people who are going to always look good on camera. Part of them looking good is you because you are the one taking care of their hair. Just thinking about this gives me goosebumps! Think about how you can so easily dance your way in front of someone else's audience.

Even though not every single one of those followers are going to want their hair done by you, statistically big and small celebrities have a 5% super-fan base. These fans will wear, go to, and do business with whoever this influencer recommends.

You might be thinking, "Do I have to give away a $300+ services?" The answer to that is YES. Here's why:

If 1% of the 1,000 people who engage with this influencer wants to come get their hair done with you after the influencer does, those are ten hot new leads that you can now charge whatever you want. Out of those ten people, three might follow through on their appointment, so at $300 per appointment, you're looking at an income of at least $900 from clients that didn't know who you were before you did that complimentary service for the influencer.

Can you see now how the numbers stack in your favor? It's just a matter of successfully connect with these influencers. The main thing is to start!

Nothing Is Free, Not Even Clients

I am asked on a daily basis, "How do I find clients for free?" When you don't have the financial resources or the marketing savvy to sustain your business long term, you must be willing to do the legwork and spend time looking for other professionals to partner with on social media. Bartering has existed for thousands of years, and as much as the economy is based on moving money around and paying for services and goods, it works just as well when you barter your time and services with people who can get eyes on your work.

Bartering may also be considered a tax write off. When you give away free services to these local mini-celebrities and well-connected individuals in your community, there is a financial opportunity cost. Some call it the cost of doing business, but the government often times calls it a business expense. Depending on where you live and how good your accountant is, you might be able to write off that influencer service you gave away for free, so that service actually saves you from paying taxes. (Please check with a professional as laws may differ from country to country).

Why can this be considered a business expense? Two words: perceived value. The influencer is a human like the rest of us, but in the online world he or she is a brand, and the larger their audience is, the higher their perceived value. Influencers are actually curators for their audiences, who depend on them to guide them towards new and improved services and products.

There is no one-size-fits-all strategy with these influencers, you have to be ready to negotiate with them individually based on how large their following is. The end result you want is them walking around with your work on their heads and their large audience exposed to your skills and talents, exponentially increases your opportunity of growing your clientele base quicker.

The influencer wins and you win long term. Everyone wins. So start spending a little bit of time on the explore page of your local hashtags and start nurturing relationships with those local mini-celebrities.

CHAPTER 21

The Role of Email in Client Retention

During my salon days, the owners I worked for had a really bad habit of spamming client emails with discounts and other useless tactics, that would eventually annoy my and everyone else's clients. I also worked for several bosses who wouldn't allow their hairstylists anywhere near the email list, the front desk, or the contact information.

I'm not ashamed to say that there was a point in my salon career where I had to take the information from the computer when the owner wasn't there. Even though I did nothing wrong, this felt uncomfortable - not because I thought I was stealing (I wasn't), but because I worked in so many salons where this was considered normal. Only a few years ago I was in a position where I had no idea where my next client was going to come from because the salon owner never marketed. I had to put up with my clients information being held hostage by someone who called themselves my boss, when he really was just a facilitator of space and product. He was a landlord, not an entrepreneur.

In this chapter, I want to focus specifically on a simple strategy for continuity once you do acquire a client. There is marketing that has to be done in order to acquire clients, but there is also a certain type of marketing that is done for the purpose of retaining clients.

So What About Email?

There are countless ways to go about utilizing email properly in order to keep your clientele happy. The number one thing I want you NOT to do is to spam your clients with discount emails. This is a race to the bottom. Clients can smell desperation from the other side of the screen.

It's one thing if you want to offer specials on a slow day or email out once or twice a month; it's another to email them every week begging them to come and see you. Think about the times in your life when you've been flirted with, you could easily tell the difference between desperation and genuine interest. Clients are the same way. They know you are running a business, it's no secret; you don't need to constantly remind them.

You need to shift your mindset from one of cheapening your services to a mindset of abundance. The way you do this is by giving free information away via email instead of begging for clients to come sit in your chair, without expectation of anything in return. I promise you that if you do this consistently, clients will show up out of nowhere. Karma is a magical and wonderful thing.

There are 24 hours in a day, and if a client spends a few hours a month in your chair, you need to be able to keep tabs on them by helping them take better care of their hair during the times they are not in your chair. If you are hellbent on sending weekly or bi-weekly emails (which you should), then make sure the emails contain valuable content.

Again, get in the client's shoes by thinking about your own behavior. You only want to read the emails that benefit you and that you get something out of. When you receive sales and discount emails, you automatically think that they are spam. Your client thinks the same way.

It is a much better strategy to send your clientele emails with information helps them and reminds them of how to better take care of their hair, as opposed to treating them like a walking dollar sign. They will appreciate you treating them with care, compassion, and without expectations.

Allow me to present to you an example from an industry much like ours - the fitness industry. Much like hairstylists, personal trainers are overworked, underpaid, and underappreciated. Similar to hairstylists, personal trainers are struggling because they are overly-focused on finding new clients, and not focused enough on teaching their clients what to do outside of the gym.

You as the hair professional have to be willing to give away your knowledge to your clients so that your clients feel that they have ways of keeping up with their hair until they visit you again. They need to know you have their back.

I laugh every time I see a hairstylist rant on social media about how their clients expect them to tell them things for free. The client pays for the physical act of the service, but you as the hair professional need to make your life easier for the next service and their life easier for the times they are not in your care in order to keep a good business relationship going. The same people that rant and put their own skills on this imaginary pedestal are the same people that go out and end up looking for a second job and then wonder why they keep losing clients. If you are reading this and are saying to yourself, "I tend to do this," please stop doing it.

You Are a Business Servant

Check your ego at the door. You are in the service business. You are a servant as much as your are a creative. If you expect to get paid for your SERVICES then you are a servant. The moment you understand that your work isn't limited to the salon environment is the moment you start to win. You want a higher income? Serve more and serve better.

If anything, you must be like your family doctor. Keep charts off your hair patients' and data and photos on what you did the previous service so you can focus on maintaining and improving their hair health. Having detailed records also helps mitigate your anxiety levels because you know exactly what you worked on last time. Ultimately it will also make you look more professional - organization is key.

Clients Hold the Money

Your job as a hairstylist, regardless of how talented you may be, is commoditized. You must stop putting your skills and talents on a pedestal, especially when it comes to email communications Again, you must understand that your role is to serve.

Serve them with helpful tips, useful videos, and valuable information. Stop using your email or text messages to pander to your own clients - its a huge turn-off. Be the artist that you set out to be. Everybody and their mother spams their clients with overplayed discount offers. If discount clients are all you expect out of your career, then that's all you are going to get.

As I'm finishing this book up, there are over a million hairstylists in the U.S. alone, and they can all more or less do what you do. Only a few thousand of those will read this book. This means that you are one of only a very few thousand hairstylists who has been offered this point of view.

Some of you will call it a radical perspective, I prefer to call it common sense in today's fast-moving business environment. You can sit there and sulk about all the wrong ways people in your career have told you to do things, or you can start doing things right today - right now.

Stop Stealing Your Clients' Time

To close off the chapter, I want to leave you with one important nugget of information. It would be nice if the next time you sent a client an email, instead of thinking about what it is that you're getting out of the deal, think about the time you are stealing away from that client.

I thought about this long and hard as I was writing this book because I didn't want to pander to you. I didn't want to tell you what you wanted to hear just to stroke your ego. You wouldn't grow from that.

Just the same, you have to offer to clients what other hairstylists aren't willing to offer. It takes practice, but whatever others are doing, you have to do the opposite. Just because you have been doing the same thing for years, it doesn't mean you can't switch it up today.

You have to adapt and be different. Think twice before you hit that send button on your emails because that client is a human being whose time you are taking away from with your communications.

CHAPTER 22

Text Messages and Trust: The Skipio Case Study

Even though we live in a social-media-driven business world, we still use text messaging to find and communicate with clients. This chapter was almost left out until I realized that wonderful platforms like Skipio that lower the amount of time we spend doing repetitive work, such as sending text messages, and compliment the new world of social media platforms.

I want to share with you my opinion on text message automation because even if you do nothing else that this book teaches, I know you are already doing the text message thing. So let's get started.

If You're Overwhelmed with Social Media and Email

I know many of you feel overwhelmed with social media posts, paid advertising, and keeping up with what seems to be an always-changing business environment. I agree that social media platforms are moving targets and admit that the feeling of always having to play catch up never goes away fully. The whole purpose of this book is to share as much specific information as possible to help you make sense of the spider web of social media.

My thoughts and opinion on social media may change over time as it evolves, but I am also not romantic about it, nor am I hung up on it enough to be delusional and think that text messaging is irrelevant. It is not.

When you strip away the glitter of social media platforms, they are all just communication devices - basically fancy text messaging platforms. The reason I like Skipio is it simply improves an everyday aspect of our lives that existed long before social media was invented.

Remember ICQ, AOL, MSN?

Those were new and inventive communication media platforms for their time. But, the communication platform that has stuck around and continues to be relevant is text messaging.

Almost all of you who read this book have clients that are old enough to remember the "good old days" of one-on-one interaction via cell phone, either calls or texts. Not all of you will create an email list of your clients, and I don't believe all of you should.

I believe that online advertising, email communication, and private messaging on social media platforms are ultimately nothing but the connector between you and the very personal phone number of your future clients. Email and social media handles have become something that we give away free in exchange for sales, discounts, and other freebies, but phone numbers are still highly valued, cherished, and protected by the owner.

As much as humans have become open with their online communications, they have become protective of the private place inside their phone known as the text message inbox. When it comes to the text message feature on their phones, humans only give their number away to others who have proven trustworthy. To give you an example, the Hairstylist

Tribe email list is in the thousands, but the Hairstylist Tribe text message list is in the hundreds.

As a hair professional, you are in luck because you are in a business where you are very intimately connected with your clients. I'm willing to bet most of them still want to communicate with you via text messaging. Yes, some of them prefer WhatsApp of Facebook Messenger, but those platforms are still inherently text messaging platforms. The clients you attract using social media, will eventually trust you enough to communicate with you primarily through text messaging. That's as personal as one can get using a Smartphone.

As you grow your clientele list and get to know them, you will see that the clients you attract via social media trust you with their personal number because you took the time to reach out using what I taught you in previous chapters. You had to work for that phone number.

Trust Is Your Destination

The more noise social media creates, the more popular hairstylists emerge, and the more of them will yell loud and clear that social media is the "end all be all." It sounds like I'm contradicting everything that I have said and done since 2014, but all I am really doing is getting ahead of the confusion in order to explain to you that, while social media isn't the end all be all, it's the "right now" vehicle of our day and this vehicle has a destination. That destination is a country called trust and this book is a map to get there.

My road map helps you get the attention of your client and keep it long enough to you find your way into their text inbox, but it's up to you to keep their attention when you get there. You can be the most talented hairstylist with the best intentions, the strongest sales skills, and the coziest hair salon. But if you don't create awareness and sustain that awareness, you are going to be outpaced by less talented local hair professionals. These other local hairstylists understand that before they can sell a client anything, they have to get their attention and keep it for a while. They have to build up the trust levels.

So What About Skipio?

There is a difference between the trust levels of clients whose attention you have on social media and the trust level of clients who grant you access to their personal cell number. After three years of building an attention base of hair professionals, I have come to the conclusion that text messaging is the king of business-to-consumer relationships and as such must be cherished.

If you have been told (as I'm sure you have) that you must post three to five times a day on social media, I'm telling you right now, do NOT text message your clients three to fives times per day, or per week even. Just because text messaging, social media DMs, and emails can all be sent to the same person, it does not mean they are equivalent. They are not.

The more personal you get with the clients you find online, the less you have to communicate with them. Even so, if you are managing a full book of clients, that time can add up. Text messaging platforms like Skipio remove the burden of having to text message your clients one by one.

Of course you have to communicate with each individual client specifically and address their own hair situation, but when you generate content such as how-to videos, text message has an almost 100% open rate. How-to videos are super valuable and will be much more appreciated by a client than a random 10% discount offer. By the time a client has enough trust to open your text messages 100% of the time, you better be communicating valuable information, not just attempting to book yourself up.

I became an instant fan of Skipio when I sent my first mass text message from my laptop to 232 hairstylists from our community, and over 80 of them responded back positively - right away. I have thousands of hairstylists emails, and the most responses I've ever received via email was around 15. Unlike email, where spam is common, text message is a holy and protected part of a clients life.

I encourage you to take a look at text message automating platforms and understand that there are ways to communicate with your clients in a way where it seems personal. The more I use text automation, the more I understand that hairstylists (aka, my clients) are spending their real time to consume the information I send them. For that reason, I communicate less often then I do via social media because I am hyper-aware of the fact that I am taking up their precious time.

Way too many hairstylists use social media and text messaging as vehicles to push their crappy discount offers often, and this leads to clients being annoyed, fatigued, and eventually turned off, no matter how talented you may be. Before you send another email blast or make another social media post, I want you to put yourself in your client's shoes and ask yourself, "Is this something I would find beneficial, or would I think it's a petty and unnecessary message?"

I know people who become annoyed when their spouse texts them too much, so imagine when a half-stranger bothers you constantly to make an appointment with them!

The Flip Side Is Under-Utilizing Texts

While you never want to spam your clients, not communicating with them is equally bad for business. When I make suggestions to the Tribe on how to communicate with clients, some hairstylists seem to find problems with every solution I offer. One of the issues that is often brought up is not having enough time.

Every human on the planet has the same 24 hours as you. Some hairstylists, and you may be one of them, always find reasons not to communicate with their clients between appointments. Some of those reasons, such as spending quality time with family, are perfectly valid.

Having said that, your clients don't really care about your personal life. In the client/professional relationship, the client only cares about what the professional can do for them. Such is the reality of being in business. You have to be able to put aside your ego and emotions and understand that you are a self-employed entrepreneur. Most hairstylists don't have a safety net the way, say government workers, do. Your business is a 24-hour thing.

Client Retention

We all have to find a balance between too much client interaction and not enough. I continue to mention Skipio, the text message automation platform, because it's a tool that helps you better manage your client relationships. I can give you all kinds of ideas on what fancy new tools to use, but there are certain things in business, like client retention, that have been around and will be around as long as humans trade services for money.

You have to remember that your client is the one holding the money bag. And the one holding the money bag always has the power in business transactions. This can be a scary concept, but don't be alarmed. This chapter isn't about catering to your clients 24/7, it's about using technology tools and good old-fashioned customer service strategies to increase the chances of keeping the clientele you have worked so hard to build.

If you continue to treat your clients in a transactional manner, they will notice and feel that all you are out to do is get their money on your own terms. Good business is built off of respect, and they will not feel respected when they feel as if they're treated like a walking dollar sign. You have to play by their rules, and the client service industry already has outlined strategies for you to grow your professional business.

You can be the most talented hairstylist in the world, but if your clients don't feel as if they're getting the most value out of their relationship with you, like in any other relationship you will get cheated on or left behind.

It's Just the Reality of Life

To recap, if you use social media to attract new clients, then you really need to use text messaging and text automation as a strategy to keep those clients. This will end up saving you more time, even though it feels like another thing to do.

You must nurture client relationships in order for them to flourish. The more you take them by the hand and help them with their hair problems, the more likely that you will keep their business.

CHAPTER 23

Next Steps

I have poured every piece of relevant information and useful advice I could fit in this book for you to consume, digest, and duplicate on your own. If you do nothing else, I want you to consider this book to be your north star for what to do inside your hair service business, in the immediate future. Don't overthink it, just start doing it. There is no perfect time, so just start!

You should also congratulate yourself, feel proud, and treat yourself. Coffee and ice-cream is my go-to treat (if you want to get fancy with it, put the ice-cream scoop IN the coffee).

I also want to congratulate you on taking massive action and reading it from start to finish. If you've made it to this page, you must know that you are now part of a small percentage of hairstylists who have been armed with this type of information and actionable steps.

Besides the straight forward and actionable advice, this book has provided you with something else: motivation and inspiration to continue pushing forward and doing everything in your power to grow your business. I want you to know that anything is possible as long as you work for it. Effort is key.

The famous author, speaker, and motivation guru Tony Robbins says that 99% of people will take the information and sit on it - they will not take action. I have to agree. This book was placed in front of thousands of hairstylists on social media, but only a handful of them took action and read it - and you are one of them.

Over the last few years, out of the tens of thousands of Hairstylist Tribe members I have communicated with, I have found around 1,000 of them to be super driven and willing to stop at nothing to achieve what they desire. These are the hair professionals I want to work and grow with. While every one of these thousands of Tribe members have the same advantage as everyone else (as long as they own a smartphone) these 1,000 hairstylists are the ones I want to impact and be there for in the future. They are the ones I want to grow with and do business with.

It took L'Oreal over 40 years to become what it is today, and it, too, started with a few thousand "allies." My goal is to work with 1,000 of you over the coming years. It is only when a person finds their Tribe that they can make an impact in their industry. We cannot go at it alone. Not for what we want to build here.

If you want to be one of our allies, if you want to put a dent in the beauty industry, I want to hear from you. Simply email me at hairstylisttribe@gmail.com with the subject line "I want to be your ally."

I would also love for you to include a picture or a selfie of you holding the book. That's the biggest compliment any author can receive. Thank you for your ongoing support and I look forward to hearing from you soon!

With love,

Melissa Liscio

Hairstylist Tribe

99235797R00105

Made in the USA
Lexington, KY
14 September 2018